The American Hiroshima: Osama's Plan for a Nuclear Attack, And One Man's Attempt to Warn America

Dr. Hugh Cort

iUniverse, Inc.
New York   Bloomington

iUniverse books may be ordered through booksellers or by contacting:

iUniverse
1663 Liberty Drive
Bloomington, IN 47403
www.iuniverse.com
1-800-Authors (1-800-288-4677)

Because of the dynamic nature of the Internet, any Web addresses or links contained in this book may have changed since publication and may no longer be valid. The views expressed in this work are solely those of the author and do not necessarily reflect the views of the publisher, and the publisher hereby disclaims any responsibility for them.

ISBN: 978-1-4401-8647-9 (sc)
ISBN: 978-1-4401-8648-6 (ebook)

Printed in the United States of America

iUniverse rev. date: 11/20/2009

Dedication

I lovingly dedicate this book to the love of my life, my wonderful, precious wife Deborah May Cort. Debbie was such a blessing to me for twenty-four great years. She went to Heaven in July 2008 after a long illness. She was, and is, my heart. She continues to comfort me and bless me, and she and Jesus are with me in spirit, and I dearly look forward to the day I can be with my sweetheart again in Heaven. I love you, Honey!

Contents

Acknowledgments

The person who has done the most to discover Osama bin Laden's American Hiroshima plan and warn America is my friend and colleague, the brilliant Dr. Paul Williams, author of five books on Osama bin Laden, al Qaeda, Iran, and their American Hiroshima plan. I would never have even known about the American Hiroshima without Paul Williams'exceptional research. His analytical skills and investigative genius are on a whole other level from everyone else. Just like Sherlock Holmes could see clues that no one else could see, even Scotland Yard, Paul Williams has "put together the pieces" and shown us "the big picture" of Osama bin Laden's plans for a devastating nuclear attack on America. Paul is Sherlock Holmes, and I am the humble Dr. Watson, his faithful side-kick, assisting him as best I can. Thank you, Dr. Williams, for your hard work and dedicated genius in bringing to light, and warning America, about the coming American Hiroshima! You are indeed, as John Kasich suggested on his "From The Heartland" TV show on Fox News, a modern day Paul Revere, warning America about the next 9/11, coming soon!

I want to thank the members of the board of my counter-terrorism think tank, the American Foundation for Counter-Terrorism Policy and Research (AFCPR.org) – General Tom McInerney, honorary board member; Dr. Paul Williams, Vice President and Board Member, Michael Travis, Board Member, Dean Allen, Treasurer and Board Member, and Laurice Tatum, Secretary and Board Member.

A special thanks to Hamid Mir for his fearless and courageous research and on-the-ground investigative journalism (who else do you know who has interviewed Osama bin Laden three times, and risked his life interviewing Taliban and Hezbollah and al Qaeda terrorists, once getting captured and mistreated by the Taliban, once getting captured and mistreated by Hezbollah in Lebanon during the Israeli-Lebanon conflict, and once having his office destroyed and being beaten by former President Musharraf's thugs, and twice in the past losing his job for exposing corruption in Pakistan.

And thanks to Yossef Bodansky, former Director of the Congressional Task Force on Terrorism (for 16 years!), and author of <u>Chechen Jihad</u>, the story of how Osama bin Laden purchased suitcase nuclear bombs on the black market that had been stolen from the former Soviet Union.

And thanks to Joseph Farah, who has brought important media investigation about the American Hiroshima in World Net Daily, which reaches eight million people a month, and Jerome Corsi, who was one of the first to bring attention to Iran's lethal nuclear plans in his ground-breaking book <u>Nuclear Iran</u>, and has now given us more crucial information with his brand new book <u>Why Israel Can't Wait</u> (to take out Iran's nuclear sites before it's too late.)

I would also like to thank my hardworking and dedicated Presidential campaign staff, that did such a great job of helping me and Dr. Williams warn America.

And, I would like to thank my hardworking typist at Systematic Services, for making this book possible. I would also like to thank my publisher, iuniverse.com, for bringing this book to the world.

And finally, I would like to thank my darling Debbie, who encouraged me when she was living, and continues to encourage me now from Heaven—I love you forever, Sweet Debbie!

Introduction

Does anyone really think that Osama bin Laden is done with America, that he is through doing terror attacks? Some people, including some in the media, have erroneously given way to wishful thinking, believing that Osama bin Laden is dead, or that he has such serious kidney problems, that he is unable to mount any threat against the Unites States, or that he is on the run, living in a cave, and broke financially, so that he is unable to effectively plan any attack. Other people tend to think that Osama, although he makes a lot of threats by audiotapes, and sometimes by videotape, is just full of hot air, and is bragging and bluffing and exaggerating, as former National Security Advisor Fran Townsend erroneously referred to him as being "impotent," and that if we believe him we are just doing what the terrorists want to accomplish, instilling fear.

However I am here to tell you Osama bin Laden is alive and well, has plenty of money, and is energetically planning his long awaited American Hiroshima attack, where he destroys ten American cities, plus London, Paris, and Rome with nuclear bombs. Our National Intelligence Agencies report that the audiotapes Osama puts out through the al Qaeda media front as–Sahab are all genuine (he just put another audiotape out a few days ago in fact), and they say there has never been a faked bin Laden tape. Although on an audiotape a year ago Osama had some noticeable shortness of breath, he sounds just fine on the recent audiotapes. Osama told Hamid Mir he was amused by Americans thinking he had severe kidney problems and was on dialysis.

He told Hamid Mir he doesn't have kidney problems.

Osama and al Qaeda have plenty of money, thanks to the huge opium operation going on in Afghanistan. Afghanistan produces 93% of the world's opium, which is transported through Taliban controlled areas of the country on its way to market in Turkey (the Taliban controls 12 of the 20 provinces in Afghanistan), where it is used to make heroin. The Taliban takes a big cut of the profits and gives a lot to al Qaeda and Osama. Also there is some evidence Osama is being sheltered in Iran, which is why we can't ever seem to find Osama. And Iran is helping Osama with financial help, and also by having nuclear scientists, Pakistani nuclear scientists who are assisting the Iranian program, to also assist Al Qaeda to "weaponize fissionable materials they have already obtained," according to British Intelligence MI6.

And for those who think Osama is bluffing, trying to scare Americans into thinking he has nuclear bombs when he really doesn't – a psychological study of Osama, and a review of all his statements, shows him to be a man of his word – when he told Al–Quds Al–Arabi newspaper he "was going to attack America in an unprecedented way for its support of Israel," three weeks later he carried out his threat to the letter in the 9/11 attacks. When Osama says he is going to do something, he means it. When he says, as he did in an audiotape "The only reason we have not attacked America yet is not because of your security precautions – it is simply that we are not quite through with our preparations," and then goes on to say, "The minute the preparations are through, you will see the attacks in your own homes," we had better take him seriously!

When Ahmadinejad of Iran says, "We will soon see a world without the United States," and leads Iranians in "Death to America" cheers, we had better take him seriously. When the top advisor to Iran's Supreme Leader Khamenei says , "We Iranians have devised a strategy for the destruction of Anglo-Saxon Civilization, and we know how we are going to attack them," we had better take him seriously. When FBI Director Robert Mueller testifies to Congress that Iran's terror network, Hezbollah, has now come across the Mexican border and is now in our country, we need to get alarmed. When FBI Director Mueller tells NewsMax that al Qaeda 'is desperately seeking nuclear weapons and nuclear materials, they have targeted New York and Washington, and I have trouble sleeping at night for worrying about a nuclear attack on America," we need to take notice. When former vice-president Dick Cheney says, "There is a high probability of a nuclear or biological attack on America in the next year," we need to take notice. And when National Security Advisor James Jones says al Qaeda is determined to do a nuclear attack on the United States we need to get on the alert. Wake up, America!!!

When I first read, in the dust jacket of Paul Williams' landmark book <u>Osama's Revenge: The Next 9/11</u> , that Osama bin Laden was planning a nuclear attack on America, and had acquired suitcase nuclear bombs which he was bringing through the Mexican border with the help of MS-13 drug smugglers, I couldn't believe it! I threw the book in a corner and refused to look at it for seven months, because of two strong feelings I had – first, it sounded like science fiction, and second, I had this terrible sinking feeling that if it was true, we are doomed, and I just didn't want to face it. So the book got covered with dust for seven months. But then I got some emails from some friends who do counter-terrorism research saying the same thing, and I thought, "I guess I had better read that book!" So I got it out of the corner, and read it, and was horrified as it dawned on me that Yes, Osama bin Laden has acquired functional suitcase nuclear bombs, and there is a high probability he is going to succeed in his American Hiroshima plan, as presented in the fatwa he obtained, to kill ten million Americans with nuclear weapons!

Later I got to meet the brilliant Paul Williams in person, and we went on several investigative trips to Canada searching for Adnan Shukrijumah, who FBI Director Robert Mueller calls "the next Mohammed Atta," the man Osama bin laden has designated to lead the next 9/11, which will be a nuclear 9/11.

Paul brought noted Pakistani journalist Hamid Mir to America, who told us about his interview with Osama bin Laden after 9/11, when Osama and Ayman al-Zawahiri, the number two man in al Qaeda, told him they had acquired suitcase nuclear bombs on the black market which had been stolen from the former Soviet Union. Then I met Yossef Bodansky, the former Director of the Congressional Task Force on Terrorism, who told me it was true Osama had acquired 20 suitcase nukes that were stolen from the former Soviet Union (see his book Chechen Jihad). Then my friend General Tom McInerney, CNN and Fox News military analyst, told me he thinks America may be hit by a nuclear attack by terrorists in a year or less. And more, and more, and more information keeps coming in. If you would like to see some of our information for yourself, just go to our website, www. afcpr.org.

To do more vital counter-terrorism work, I founded the American Foundation for Counter-Terrorism Policy and Research, a 501(c)(3) nonprofit counter-terrorism think tank. General Tom McInerney is an honorary board member. Dr. Paul Williams is a board member, as is Michael Travis, who has ties to Israel's Intelligence agency Mossad. Laurice Tatum, a private investigator who has worked with the FBI, is on the board. And Dean Allen, who is a leading candidate for Adjutant General of the South Carolina State Guard, is on our board. Some people may say, "How can private citizens do counter-terrorism research? Why not leave it up to the CIA and FBI?" USA Today newspaper, on the front page, had a story about open source intelligence (open source means it is not classified – anyone can find it on the internet and elsewhere) and how 90% of the intelligence the CIA and the FBI get is open source, and how the CIA and the FBI really should spend more time on open source, for example looking at jihadi terrorist websites, than waiting for dribbles of classified information from paid informants who may be making things up just to get paid. CNN said the same thing a few days later. And we can't "just leave it up to the CIA and the FBI." After all, they let us down on 9/11, and they are letting us down on Osama bin Laden's coming American Hiroshima nuclear attack!

Remember, the 9/11 Commission said in its report that had the FBI told the media and the public about the warning signs they had about 9/11 prior to 9/11, there was a good chance we may have been able to stop 9/11! And now the same thing is happening all over again! My goal is to get the news that Osama bin laden is far along in his plan for a devastating nuclear attack on America out into the media, so the media will do a thorough investigation, and warn the American people, so that maybe we can stop Osama's American Hiroshima, or, if we can't stop it, we can at least tell millions of Americans how to avoid deadly radiation sickness. I saw a poll where 66% of Americans think that Osama bin Laden will attack America again, and this time, it will be a nuclear attack. Unfortunately, they are probably right. I have written this book to try to stop Osama's American Hiroshima. To learn more how you can help, please read the rest of this book!

Chapter One

The American Hiroshima: Osama bin Laden's Plan for a Nuclear Attack

Osama bin Laden has been working diligently ever since 1992 on his "American Hiroshima" plan to destroy seven to ten American cities with nuclear devices. He first began seeking enriched uranium in 1992, and there is considerable evidence that he has finally finished preparations for his life work, his "Grand Finale," his "American Hiroshima," and is now just waiting for the right moment to pull the trigger and devastate multiple American cities in an attack that will make the destruction of 9/11 seem insignificant by comparison. In September, 2008, ABC News reported that our Intelligence agencies had intercepted a message from al Qaeda High Command to local al Qaeda cells around the world saying, "Be on notice, we may call upon you soon."[1] Then, a few months later, five days after the American Presidential election, on Nov. 9, 2008 al-Quds Al-Arabi newspaper, an Arabic newspaper, published on the front page that Osama bin Laden has now given the order for and set in motion a new, huge attack on America that will be "far bigger than 9/11" and that will "change the economic and political structure of the world" and will take place "in the near future."[2] Al-Quds Al-Arabi is the same newspaper that three weeks before 9/11 published a statement from Osama saying he was "going to attack America in an unprecedented way." Three weeks later, he did 9/11. Now the same newspaper is saying that Osama has ordered a new, huge attack on America!

Let us look at the progression of Osama's plan. In 1996 he issues his "Declaration of War Against the Americans Occupying the Land of the Two Holy Places." Later, he obtains a fatwa, or religious order, from an Islamic cleric saying it is permissible to kill 4 million

Americans, and 2 million of those need to be children for the sake of parity (Osama says since Americans are directly or indirectly responsible for 2 million Muslim children dying, 2 million American children must die). Then, as Christiane Amanpour reports in her CNN TV Special "In the Footsteps of bin Laden," in 2003 Osama obtains his "nuclear fatwa" from Saudi cleric Nasir Bin Hamid Al-Fahd, granting al Qaeda permission to kill 10 million Americans with nuclear weapons! And now the number of American children that must be killed for the sake of parity has been upgraded by Osama to 3 million!

Has Osama obtained functional nuclear weapons? I interviewed Hamid Mir, the noted Pakistani journalist who has interviewed Condoleeza Rice, Tony Blair, and former Pakistani President Musharraf. Hamid Mir is the most well-known of all the journalists in Pakistan, and is anchor of GEO TV News, the most popular TV news station in Pakistan. Hamid Mir came to America to speak at a counter-terrorism convention, and I was able to interview him in person. Hamid Mir has interviewed Osama bin Laden three times, and he is the only person who interviewed Osama after 9/11 (in November of 2001, just before Osama fled Afghanistan through Tora Bora). Hamid told me, and he has told this to others as well, including Glenn Beck, that Osama told him, and Ayman al-Zawahiri told him also (Ayman al-Zawahiri is al Qaeda's second-in-command), that they had acquired suitcase nuclear bombs on the black market that had been stolen from the former Soviet Union. As Ayman al-Zawahiri told Hamid Mir, "If you go to BBC reports, you will find that thirty nuclear weapons are missing from Russia's nuclear arsenal. We have links with Russia's underworld channels." He went on to say, "If you have $30 million, go to the black market in central Asia, contact any disgruntled Soviet scientist, and a lot of...smart briefcase bombs are available. They have contacted us, we sent our people to Moscow, to Tashkent, to other central Asian states and they negotiated, and we purchased some nuclear bombs."[3]

Stewart Stogel, who has worked for *Time Magazine* and other noted publications, has extensively interviewed Hans Blix, the former Director General of the IAEA, the United Nations' International Atomic Energy Agency. In 2004, Stogel reported in NewsMax that Hans Blix was asked by the IAEA to investigate reports that Osama bin Laden had acquired 20 suitcase nuclear bombs that were stolen from the former Soviet Union. Hans Blix interviewed the Russian officials who reported the theft of the bombs, and he interviewed the Chechen Muslim rebels who had stolen the bombs and sold them to Osama, and Hans Blix concluded that Osama bin Laden had indeed acquired 20 suitcase nuclear bombs, and he made a report of this to his colleagues at the IAEA.[4]

Yossef Bodansky, who was the Director of the U.S. Congress's Task Force on Terrorism for 16 years, writes in his book Chechen Jihad about the Chechen Muslim rebels who stole the suitcase nukes from the former Soviet Union and sold them to Osama. I personally asked Yossef, "Is it true what Hamid Mir is saying, that Osama has acquired suitcase nukes that were stolen from the former Soviet Union?" and he replied, "Yes it is true, and it is in my book also." In Chechen Jihad Yossef goes on to say that Osama also hired former

Soviet SPESNAZ special forces soldiers whose job it had been in the former Soviet Union to maintain and service the suitcase nukes for the KGB, to maintain them for Osama (the suitcase nukes need maintenance about every 6 months), and they were able to "hotwire" the nukes so they could be detonated by a terrorist and bypass the activation code from Moscow.[5]

Khalid Sheikh Mohammed, Osama's master-planner for 9/11, when he was captured told the Pakistani Intelligence and the CIA (and it was on his laptop computer as well, so we know this wasn't just waterboarded out of him) that Osama bin Laden is planning a "nuclear hellstorm" for America, and he is targeting seven main cities, with three additional cities he may include. The targeted cities he mentioned were New York, Washington, Boston, Miami, Houston, Las Vegas, Los Angeles, Philadelphia, Chicago, and the Valdez, Alaska, the biggest oil terminal in America. The first seven cities are named as the main target cities, and the last three are named as possible additions.[6] For the rest of this book, we will refer to "the ten cities" Osama has targeted, because there is a good chance he will hit all ten, and not just seven; in fact, since it has been six years since Khalid Sheikh Mohammed was captured and named the target cities, it may be that Osama and Iran have added even more cities to the target list. It should be noted also, as we will explain later in this book, Osama also plans to detonate nuclear bombs in London, Paris, Rome, and possibly also Copenhagen and other European cities at the same time he does the American Hiroshima--remember that an Iranian leader said Iran has already picked out 37 sites to attack in America and elsewhere "in the West," meaning European countries who are allied with America.

Osama, funded by proceeds from the huge opium trade in Afghanistan, has purchased enriched uranium on the black market in addition to his 20 suitcase nukes. Afghanistan produces 93% of the world's opium, which has to go through Taliban-controlled areas on its way to market in Turkey. The Taliban takes a huge cut of the enormous profits, and gives a lot of it to Osama and al Qaeda, in addition to funding its war on U.S. and NATO troops in Afghanistan, and its assault on Pakistan. As noted author and counter-terrorism researcher Paul Williams points out in his blog www.thelastcrusade.org, our troops have been told not to interfere with the opium farmers, because it will turn the farmers against the U.S. and NATO troops. Several years ago, the U.S. Congress voted against spraying the Afghan poppy fields, because Afghan President Karzai had begged them not to, because he said the farmers need it for money, and it would turn them against the government. It should be noted that President Karzai's brother is a big drug dealer and king-pin! Gretchen Peters has also written a very noteworthy book, Seeds of Terror, on how the Afghan poppies bring millions of dollars to the Taliban and al Qaeda. So here we are, enabling the production of 93% of the world's opium that is used to fund terrorists who are planning for the destruction of America! So Osama bin Laden, instead of being broke and on the run, actually has millions of dollars with which to purchase nuclear material, and hire former Soviet nuclear scientists, and scientists from other countries, to help him develop his nuclear bomb program! And he has been assisted by Dr. A. Q. Khan, father of Pakistan's nuclear bomb, and is presently being assisted by Iran and six renegade Pakistani nuclear scientists that are also helping Iran develop its nuclear bomb, as we shall see.[7]

Former Director of the CIA, George Tenet, wrote in his book <u>At the Center of the Storm: My Years at the CIA</u> that two Pakistani nuclear scientists who helped Pakistan develop its nuclear bomb, were in Afghanistan with Osama bin Laden and his second-in-command, Ayman al-Zawahiri three weeks before 9/11, helping Osama with his nuclear program![8] These nuclear scientists, Dr. Bashiruddin Mahmoud and Dr. Choudry Majid, later went to Iran, where they and four other Pakistani nuclear scientists have been helping Iran with its nuclear program. And, according to French terrorism expert Alexander Cirilovic, as reported by Irish counter-terrorism expert Gordon Thomas in World Net Daily's G-2 Intelligence Bulletin, in 2006 Britain's intelligence agency MI 6 said these Pakistani nuclear scientists "have been assisting al Qaeda to weaponize fissionable material it has already obtained."[9] The hard part about making a nuclear weapon is obtaining the fissionable material, enriched uranium. Once you have that, making the bomb is relatively simple. A ten kiloton nuclear bomb is simply a pipe with enriched uranium at one end as a target, and enriched uranium at the other end as a bullet, with an explosive charge behind the bullet that, when set off, propels the uranium "bullet" into the uranium "target," which causes the nuclear fission reaction and explosion of the bomb. The fact that al Qaeda has fissionable material (enriched uranium), and that skilled Pakistani nuclear scientists, who developed Pakistan's nuclear bomb, have been helping al Qaeda develop its nuclear bomb since 2006 or earlier, should put a chill in anyone's heart!

So there is evidence that al Qaeda has nuclear devices, probably already brought into America with the help of drug smugglers through the porous Mexican border. Our border patrol has found over 34 tunnels the drug smugglers have dug underneath the Mexican border. One of these tunnels, shown on CNN's 360 show by Anderson Cooper, cost an estimated million dollars to build, had electricity, lights, and air conditioning, and was big enough to drive a truck through! Our border patrol catches about 12,000 SIA's, or Special Interest Aliens every year who have illegally crossed the border. Special Interest Aliens are not Mexicans or South Americans. They are aliens from terror-connected countries such as Iran, Iraq, Syria, Sudan, Egypt, Pakistan, Yemen, and Saudi Arabia.[10] Where are these aliens getting the thousands of dollars needed to come to Mexico from the Middle East, and then pay coyotes, the drug smugglers who also transport illegals across the border, thousands of dollars for passage? A prominent Islamic cleric has stated that thousands of sleeper agents have been brought into the U.S. so they can play their role when the time comes for Osama's American Hiroshima. And what does our border patrol do when they catch these suspicious Middle Eastern Islamic illegals from terrorist-connected countries? They let them go! There are not enough jail cells to hold them, so they are given notices to return for trial in a month or so, and released, in the famous (or infamous) "Catch and Release" program!

To add to our worries, it appears Iran is even more actively assisting Osama in his American Hiroshima plan than just providing Pakistani nuclear scientists to weaponize al Qaeda's fissionable material (enriched uranium) into nuclear bombs. FBI Director Robert Mueller testified to Congress that Iran's terror network, Hezbollah, has come through the Mexican border and is now here in America! In fact, in his book <u>American Hiroshima: The Reasons Why and a Call to Strengthen America's Democracy</u> author David Dionisi reports that Iran is pursuing their own American Hiroshima plan, and now they have merged their plan with Osama's![11] So now the world's most dangerous terrorist, the evil genius Osama bin Laden, is teamed up with the biggest terror-sponsoring nation in the world, Iran!

Have you ever wondered why Ahmadinejad and the Mullahs are so bold in pursuing their nuclear program, despite sanctions and threats from the United Nations and most civilized countries of the world? Do you know that Ahmadinejad continually gives speeches saying "We will soon see a world without the United States?" Did you see the huge outdoor rally covered on C-SPAN, where Ahmadinejad led thousands of Iranians in chanting "Death to America! Death to America"?

Do you know that Iran's first goal is to destroy America (which it calls the Big Satan) and then destroy Israel (the Little Satan)? The media tries to minimize the threat from Ahmadinejad, saying in effect "Ahmadinejad is aggressive, but not to worry, he is under the control of the Mullahs." Do you know that one of the top advisors to the head Mullah himself, Supreme Leader Khamenei, said "We Iranians have devised a strategy for the destruction of Western Civilization, and we know how we are going to attack them!" Do you know that a high up leader in Iran said, "We already have 37 sites picked out for attack in America and elsewhere in the West"? When seven to ten, or more, American cities go up in nuclear mushroom clouds in the near future, remember, it was not just Osama, but Iran assisting him, that did it.

And it is not just nuclear bombs going off in our cities we have to worry about. The attack will also include biological attacks with deadly anthrax, chemical attacks, Mumbai-style assaults with Ak-47's by al Qaeda and Hezbollah and Jamaat-ul-Fuqra terrorists living right here in America, Beslan-style attacks on our schools, and, possibly worse of all, EMP attacks (Electromagnetic Pulse attacks), where an Iranian ship (there are hundreds of Iranian ships in our Great Lakes as we speak, sailing under "flags of convenience" of other countries like Panama), could fire a nuclear missile miles above earth, where it detonates, causing an electomagnetic pulse of gamma rays that knock out all electrical circuits over a wide area of America.

As David Dionisi explains in his book <u>American Hiroshima: The Reasons Why and a Call to Strengthen America's Democracy</u>, another facet of Osama's and Iran's multi-pronged American Hiroshima attack may be to have small planes carry nukes and detonate above or into some of our nuclear reactors, causing a "force multiplier effect"-- a huge nuclear explosion, that will disperse into the atmosphere tons of "highly radioactive nuclear power plant fuel and waste. The initial explosion would certainly kill many people. The subsequent downwind radioactive fallout, traveling from the nuclear power plant for hundreds of miles downwind, could kill millions of Americans."[12] Dionisi goes on to say that Khalid Sheikh Mohammed, Osama's chief planner for 9/11, revealed to the CIA that although "senior al Qaeda leaders wanted to include nuclear power plants in the 9/11 attacks," Osama was "unyielding in his opposition to crashing airplanes into nuclear power plants," and wanted nuclear facilities to be left alone, "for now." As Dionisi cogently explains, Osama's "for now" "is significant because if al Qaeda did not crash airplanes into nuclear facilities, Osama calculated [correctly] that the U.S. Government would not harden these targets," and he would be able later, in the future American Hiroshima attack, to use nuclear weapons to hit nuclear power plants and cause much more destruction than just a crashed airplane would.[13] Osama's uncanny way that he is saving his "big guns" for the coming American Hiroshima attack is also reflected in former CIA Director George Tenet's report that when Ayman al-Zawahiri (Osama's right hand man, second in command of al Qaeda) told an al Qaeda cell in New York that wanted to kill 3,000 Americans in the New York subways with poison gas, to stop their plan, because "We have something a lot bigger in mind," meaning the nuclear, and biological and chemical and ground troop assault plans of the coming American Hiroshima. Osama is saving it all for "The Big One," his American Hiroshima!

Let us take a look at the threat progression. Christiane Amanpour, in her CNN TV documentary "In the Footsteps of bin Laden," said that Osama took it to heart when some Muslim scholars criticized him after 9/11 for not following Islamic law, which requires you to warn an enemy, offer him a truce, and give him a chance to convert to Islam before you strike him. He then offered England and Europe a truce – when they rejected it, he did the London July 7 bombings. Now he has offered America a truce.

He has also given us warning. In his January 19, 2006 audiotape, Osama said, "The only reason we have not attacked America yet is not because of your security precautions – it is simply that we are not quite through with our preparations." Then he went on to say, "The operations are under preparation and you will see them in your homes the minute the preparations are through." Ayman al-Zawahiri and Adam Gadahn, the American al Qaeda, appear soon after in a videotape urging Americans to convert to Islam. Then Ayman al-Zawahiri says, ominously, "Now we have fulfilled all the requirements of Islamic Law – Osama has given you many warnings, he has offered you a truce, and he has given you the chance to convert to Islam. Now we are justified in attacking you."

Then, in September of 2006, Hamid Mir, the Pakistani journalist who interviewed Osama three times, was summoned to Afghanistan, where he met with the top al Qaeda commander in Afghanistan, Abu Dawood. Abu Dawood told Hamid Mir "Tell all the Muslims they must leave America now, especially New York and Washington, because Osama has completed his cycle of warnings, his preparations are through, and he may attack America at any time. This is their last warning." Hamid Mir told us that there had been a disagreement in the Shura, or Inner Council, of al Qaeda – half the members wanted to go ahead an attack America, but the other half were concerned that many Muslims will die in the attack. So Abu Dawood's warning for the Muslims to leave America was a way for the Shura to resolve this problem. Abu Dawood went on to talk about Adnan Shukrijumah, the man FBI Director Robert Mueller has called "the next Mohammed Atta," the man Osama has chosen to lead the next attack on America.

Who, you may ask, is Adnan Shukrijumah? One technical problem Osama bin Laden has had to solve in planning his multiple nuclear attacks on American cities is that suitcase nukes need to be serviced and maintained approximately every six months, primarily to keep their triggers functional. Whoever is in charge of this needs to have training and skill in nuclear technology. Also it would help to have a person who is an American citizen, who does not need a visa to enter and leave America at will. Who better than Adnan Shukrijumah, son of Islamic radical preacher Gulshair Shukrijumah, trained in nuclear technology? The FBI calls him "the next Mohammed Atta," the person Osama bin Laden has designated to lead the next 9/11, the coming American Hiroshima, just as Mohammed Atta was the leader of the original 9/11 attack. You can find out more about Adnan Shukrijumah on my old website, www.stopdoomsday.com, or on my new website, www.afcpr.org, where you can see Adnan's mugshot on his most-wanted FBI poster, with a 5 million dollar reward over his head for anyone whose information leads to his arrest. The FBI has been looking for him for over five years, but has not been able to find the ring-leader of Osama's coming attack on America.

My goal is to get more media and Congressional investigation of Osama bin Laden's American Hiroshima plan. The 9/11 Commission said in its report that if the FBI had shared the warnings they had about 9/11 prior to 9/11 with the media and the public, there is a good chance we might have been able to stop 9/11. For example, if the FBI had told the media they had captured Zacarias Moussaoui, a suspicious Muslim with terrorist ties, who was reported by his flight trainers in the flight school he attended that he wanted to fly airplanes in mid-air, but did not want to learn how to land or take-off, flight trainers all over the country would have reported their suspicious Middle Eastern Muslim flight students. Why, I was shocked to find out from my friend, a Birmingham judge, that two of the 9/11 pilots learned how to fly airplanes at a flight school right here in a suburb, Bessemer, of my hometown Birmingham!

We need to tell the American people and the media about the great danger that is coming our way – Osama bin Laden and Iran's American Hiroshima nuclear attack! We can't trust our lives to our FBI and CIA and other intelligence agencies – even if they were more competent than they are, it is just too hard for them to spot one or two secretive plotters, who may not even be Middle Eastern, but may be English or American converts to Islam, whereas 300 million Americans could possibly break the case! Nuclear expert Stephen Younger, who was in charge of nuclear weapons research at the Los Alamos National Laboratory, writes in his book The Bomb, "Unfortunately, experience tells us that we cannot rely on our intelligence agencies – which have been surprised time and again over the past decades-- to give us advance warning of an impending nuclear attack."[14]

One very important reason we need to inform the American people and the media is to get Adnan Shukrijumah's face on "America's Most Wanted" TV show. I was able to get his face on there for one night, but one night is not enough! There are only 12,000 FBI agents in America, so no wonder they have not been able to find Adnan Shukrijumah these past five years, for he is a master of disguise. But if his face were on America's Most Wanted TV show for a while, 300 million Americans and 36 million Canadians (Adnan is based in the Toronto area and makes frequent trips to the United States to lead his small team of terrorists who maintain the nukes) could find him in two weeks!

However, the media is very reluctant to touch the story of Osama's American Hiroshima plan, for fear they will "alarm the public." They are afraid to even investigate the subject! They could do an article, for example, saying "We do not know if Osama has obtained functional nuclear weapons, but we know he has been pursuing this plan for many years, so let's carefully look at and evaluate the evidence that suggests he may have succeeded in his goal." Instead, they whistle in the dark, unwilling even to examine the subject. Dr. Paul Williams and I met with Glenn Beck for 45 minutes, giving Glenn the important information we have, including one of Dr. Williams' landmark books on the subject, The Al Qaeda Connection. Glenn, to his credit, has interviewed Hamid Mir, and has had Hamid on his show several times, and has put Adnan Shukrijumah's face on the show one time to ask people to find him, along with one of his aliases, Jafar the Pilot (Adnan is an accomplished pilot, had flight training alongside Mohammed Atta, and was going to be one of the 9/11 pilots until Osama took him aside and chose him to lead the American Hiroshima). But the networks would not let Glenn talk about or explore the nuclear attack Osama was planning, the American Hiroshima, even though Hamid Mir had told him all about it. Glenn repeatedly asked us, "I need meat. Can you give me some meat?" meaning, "Do you have concrete evidence so I can talk about this on TV?" We told him in the intelligence world you don't always get concrete evidence, but you get lots of little pieces that when you put them together you see the big picture, and believe us, the big picture is pretty alarming, and certainly bears investigation. You won't see concrete evidence until the bombs go off!

It seems to me very ironic that we are not allowed to talk about Osama's American Hiroshima now, but after it happens we'll be talking about it for a hundred years! I think the American public could handle it, and if we had a full scale media investigation, we could find out how far along Osama is in his avowed plan to kill ten million Americans in a nuclear attack. If he is not very far along, we can relax (just a little), and if it is found he does have functional nuclear suitcase bombs, we, with all the 300 million Americans in our country, can possibly stop the attack! If the FBI and CIA had protected us from the first 9/11, we could possibly leave it up to them. But since they let us down on 9/11, and I guarantee they'll let us down on the American Hiroshima, I think we need to inform the public and the media and the Congress and get everyone involved in saving America! How is the FBI going to stop two Muslim extremists, who may not even be Middle Eastern in appearance, but may be English or American converts to Islam, from moving in the middle of the night a suitcase size bomb, or even a larger steamer trunk size bomb, from the basement of a non-descript house in a Washington suburb, into the trunk of a car, or the inside of a van, which they will drive in the morning and detonate a block or two from the Capitol? But if everyone in America is looking out for this, it could possibly be stopped.

For those that say, "Let the FBI handle it," I would like to remind them that even though the FBI is attempting to infiltrate mosques, and recruit informants, this may not help much, because Osama bin Laden is an extremely shrewd planner, and he is likely to keep to a very small number the team of attackers, just like he did 9/11, to minimize the possibility of discovery. In the 9/11 attack, not even the muscle hijackers knew they were going to crash the airplanes until minutes before they boarded, if indeed they were even told then. Only the eight pilots knew the full plan.

Dr. Paul Williams writes in The Day of Islam, "Khalid Sheikh Mohammed went on to say that Adnan Shukrijumah represents a "single-cell"-- a lone agent capable of launching a solo nuclear or radiological attack on a major American city. The news of such a cell reportedly startled U.S.officials, who assumed that al Qadea cells contained several members who were supported by broad logistical backup crews."[15] Just like 9/11, when only Mohammed Atta and the other seven pilots knew the whole plan, all Adnan needs are a few agents to hide the nukes in each of the ten cities – such a small cell, of dedicated al Qaeda terrorists, will be extremely difficult to penetrate, to find the nukes. The vast armies of thousands of jihadis of al Qadea, Hezbollah, and Jamaat-ul-Fuqra, who are here in America won't know where the bombs are hidden, but will just be told their marching orders to attack just before the American Hiroshima goes off, so no one will "spill the beans."

The FBI and Homeland Security are so worried about Osama's coming attack that they have spent 400 million dollars on nuclear radiation detectors which they have placed around the mosques in the ten cities Khalid Sheikh Mohammed said Osama is targeting for his American Hiroshima attack (New York, Washington, D.C., Boston, Miami, Houston, Las Vegas, Los Angeles, Philadelphia, Chicago, and Valdez, Alaska). They have also put these radiation detectors in traffic intersections and traffic "chokepoints" in Washington and New York. But lest you be comforted by this, I regret to inform you that, as Steve Coll points out in his front page article in the March 12, 2007 New Yorker Magazine,[16] these nuclear radiation detectors cannot detect enriched uranium that is shielded in lead! And of course, if these terrorists have a nuclear device they are going to have it in a lead container or shield! We just don't have the technology to see enriched uranium shielded by lead. We can see plutonium that is shielded by lead, but not enriched uranium.

So, if Osama does have functional nuclear devices already in the United States, when he is going to "pull the trigger" and detonate the devices? Many people have asked, including

Fred Barnes of Fox News and the Weekly Standard, "If Osama has nukes, why hasn't he used them already?" I would say, "Because he is waiting for exactly the right moment in history." Hamid Mir's interview of the top al Qaeda Commander in Afghanistan, mentioned above, indicated that Osama has now completed his preparations, since Muslims are warned to "leave America, especially New York and Washington, since Osama may attack America at any time, we are not saying what time" and "This is their last warning." So what is Osama waiting for? David Dionisi writes in his book American Hiroshima: The Reasons Why and a Call to Strengthen America's Democracy, "Osama bin Laden is very conscious of how history will view his "American Hiroshima"... He is fully aware that killing millions of people, especially children, can hurt the long-term growth of his movement..."[17] Osama is waiting for a "galvanizing event" as Paul Williams puts it, a defining moment in history when it will appear to the "ummah," or world body of Muslims, that he is justified in killing millions of Americans. We believe this triggering event is going to be when Israel attacks Iran's nuclear sites, which will probably happen by the end of this year, or sooner. Hamid Mir has spoken with Taliban chieftains who think this is the event that will trigger Osama's American Hiroshima. And there is evidence that Osama may be in Iran, possibly not allowed to leave Iran, and that Iran is controlling him, possibly by threatening to kill him and his children, if he were to detonate his nuclear devices in America before Ahmadinejad and the Mullahs are ready. Iran may want to wait until the last minute, to give them as much time to develop their nuclear arsenal as possible, knowing that when American cities go up in nuclear mushroom clouds there is a good possibility America may retaliate by blowing up Tehran and Qom (the "Holy City" where the Mullahs live). However, when Israel attacks Iran's nuclear facilities, the Mullahs may at that point believe they have nothing left to lose, and will let Osama pull the trigger on the American Hiroshima, while they hunker down in their deep tunnel bunkers and hope for the best.

This may seem suicidal, but the Iranian Mullahs and Ahmadinejad, and Osama bin Laden are religious fanatics, and to them it is glorious to die as martyrs for radical Islam, so they can go to Muslim heaven and get their 72 virgins! Also, their fanatical views must be understood in the context of their belief in the coming of the "Mahdi." As Paul Williams so eloquently describes in his newest book on this subject, The Day of Islam: The Annihilation of America and the Western World, the radical Islamists believe that if they can bring about a large-scale slaughter of infidels, this will usher in the coming of the "Mahdi," or "Twelfth Imam" from the sky who will rule over a world totally controlled by Islam: hence the term "Day of Islam." So Osama's and Iran's American Hiroshima attack will fulfill their fanatical religious goal to usher in the global Islamic Caliphate, and the return of the Mahdi and bring about "the Day of Islam."[18]

Let us examine further the evidence that Iran and Osama bin Laden are teaming up on the American Hiroshima. David Dionisi writes in his book American Hiroshima: The Reason Why and a Call to Strengthen America's Democracy, "The Qods Force, or

Jerusalem Force is the most secret of the Iranian regime's numerous military and intelligence organizations. Responsible for extraterritorial operations, this military unit is Iran's most active, skilled, and elite force." Dionisi goes on to say, "The Qods Force is responsible for gathering information required for targeting and attack planning and has already developed a plan to introduce and detonate nuclear weapons and other mass destruction weapons in the United States. This is why Iran has had Qods Force operatives in the United States, many of whom have been undercover for over a decade." He goes on to say that Saad bin Laden, Osama's son, who recently was reported killed in a U.S. predator drone airstrike in Pakistan, has been working for years with a small group of al Qaeda and Iranian leaders working inside Iran.[19]

Dionisi also makes a good point that Osama bin Laden is probably considering detonating a nuclear bomb in a nuclear power plant, thus creating a nuclear "force-multiplier" which not only would devastate the area around the blast, but "the subsequent downwind radioactive fallout, traveling from the nuclear power plant for hundreds of miles downwind, could kill millions of Americans and make it unsafe to live in large regions of the country." Also, a nuclear blast creates radioactive iodine, which can cause thyroid cancer 300 miles from the blast site! How would such an attack take place? A small airplane could drop a nuclear bomb on top of a nuclear power plant very easily. Congressman Curt Weldon, in his book Countdown to Terror reports that an al Qaeda cell was captured in Canada plotting to crash an airplane into the Seabrook nuclear power plant in New Hampshire, which is only 40 miles from Boston, which could have exposed millions of people to radiation poisoning. And in 2005, as the BBC reported, terrorists were arrested planning to attack the Lucas Heights nuclear facility, which is only 25 miles from Sydney, Australia.[20]

There is a strong possibility that Osama's American Hiroshima will not only be a nuclear attack, but a chemical, biological, and assault troops, Mumbai-style attack as well. In addition, there may also be an EMP attack (electro-magnetic pulse attack). Osama has said in the past that he has chemical weapons, and there is evidence he has biological weapons as well, including anthrax. An al Qaeda leader was bragging several months ago that al Qaeda may bring a suitcase full of anthrax through one of the many tunnels drug smugglers have dug underneath the Mexican border, and that this anthrax could, if dispersed properly in a big city, kill 300,000 Americans. This was reported by Sara Carter of the Washington Times. FBI Director Robert Mueller issued a report warning that terrorists could stage "Mumbai-style" attacks, where terrorists swarm out and start spraying people with assault rifles, like they did in Mumbai, India, where over 200 people were killed.

A Saudi official has warned that five thousand al Qaeda "sleeper agents" are already in the U.S. waiting for Osama to issue the order for their activation. We know that 12,000 SIA's or "Special Interest Aliens," illegal aliens from terrorism-associated countries like Pakistan, Yemen, Iran, Saudi Arabia, and Egypt, come across our border from Mexico every year and are let go in the "Catch and Release" program where illegals are captured, then released because there are not enough holding facilities to keep them. And we know that our FBI in August of 2008 intercepted messages sent from al Qaeda High Command to all the local al Qaeda cells around the world saying, "Be on notice. We may call upon you soon."[1] And we know that on Nov. 9, 2008, the Arabic newspaper Al-Quds Al-Arabi published on the front page that Osama bin Laden has now ordered a new attack on America that "will be far bigger than 9/11" and that "will change the economic and political structure of the world" and that will "take place in the near future."[2]

As mentioned previously, Al-Quds Al-Arabi is the same newspaper that three weeks before 9/11 published a statement from Osama saying he was going to attack America, and three weeks later, 9/11 happened. The article also says that Osama is ordering his various training camps around the world to step up training and they are entering a "pro-active phase."

Which brings us to the terrorist training camps that al Qaeda has right here in America! It may be a shock for many people to learn that there are terrorist paramilitary training camps right here in America, just like the al Qaeda camp in Afghanistan where we see the often-shown news clip of the al Qaeda jihadis in their ninja suits swinging from the monkey bars! There are 34 of these Jamaat-ul-Fuqra paramilitary training compounds in states all across America! Jamaat-ul-Fuqra has strong ties with al Qaeda. My colleague, mentor, and fellow board member of the American Foundation for Counter-Terrorism Policy and Research (AFCPR – website www.AFCPR.org), Dr. Paul Williams, did the original research on these Jamaat-ul-Fuqra terrorist training camps in the U.S. for Martin Mawyer's Christian Action Network, which has expanded the research and done a good job getting it out to the public. Martin Mawyer's blockbuster DVD, "Homegrown Jihad: The Terrorist Camps Around the U.S." shows a clip from an actual terrorist training video where Islamic radical terrorists are training new jihadi recruits in guerrilla warfare, at camps right here in America! The FBI knows about these camps and is doing nothing about them! As Paul Williams writes in "Springtime in Islamberg," at the 70 acre Jamaat-ul-Fuqra compound in upstate New York called Islamberg, neighbors report gunfire at all hours of the day and night, and the noise of large explosions going off (they are experimenting with IED's!). Many of the residents of Jammaat–ul–Fuqra's Islamberg have been in trouble for weapons charges. At the Best Street Mosque, in Buffalo, New York, Douglas Hagmann, director of the Northeast Intelligence Network has video of Islamic jihadis doing paramilitary training, climbing in their ninja-like suits up and across the roof of the building!

So who runs these Jamaat-ul-Fuqra paramilitary training camps? (Remember, Jamaat-ul-Fuqra is strongly related to al Qaeda) None other than known terrorist Sheikh Mubarak Ali Gilani of Pakistan. Sheikh Gilani, who has strong ties to al Qaeda, operates 24 terrorist training camps in Pakistan. In 1980, he extended his reach to America, where he established Islamberg, on a 70 acre compound in Hancock, New York, the first of 34 paramilitary jihadi training camps across America. Who lives and trains in these camps? Mostly black

Muslims who were converted in prison to Islam, and promised free shelter in the camps. As Paul Williams writes in The Day of Islam, "Gilani stated that the purpose of his group [Jamaat-ul-Fuqra] is to 'purify' Islam through violence." Williams goes on to say there are Jamaat-ul-Fuqra camps in Deposit, New York; Hyattsville, Maryland; Red House, Virginia; Falls Church, Virginia; Macon, Georgia; York, South Carolina; Dover, Tennessee; Talahina, Oklahoma; Tulane County, California; Commerce, California; Onalaska, Washington; and many other locations. Williams continues, "Gilani also instituted the International Quranic Open University as an educational arm of Jamaat-ul-Fuqra. Every year, the university sends scores of American Muslims to Pakistan reportedly for guerrilla training." Then they return to America and train others back in the camps.[23] To fly lower under the radar, Jamaat-ul-Fuqra nows calls itself by a new name, Muslims of America. So here we have FBI Director Robert Mueller warning that home-grown terrorists in the U.S. may rise up and do Mumbai-style attacks (like when 10 Islamic radicals with assault rifles sprayed bullets in public places in Mumbai, India and killed over 200 people), and we have the terrorists training right here under our noses! They will play their part in Osama's American Hiroshima attack, along with al Qaeda and Hezbollah terrorists who have come illegally across the Mexican border (the thousands of "Special Interest Aliens," illegals from terrorism-associated countries, who have been captured, and then released into our country by our Border Patrol's "Catch and Release" program). These terrorists will swarm out with semi-automatics and assault rifles into our suburbs right after the suitcase nukes destroy the downtown areas of the ten cities targeted by Osama, spraying bullets into our citizens in an orgy of violence. As Adam Gadahn, the "American al Qaeda" says, "The streets of Los Angeles will run red with blood!"

In addition to the nuclear, biological, chemical, and terrorist assault team attacks on the day of Osama bin Laden's and Iran's American Hiroshima attack, which the Al-Quds Al-Arabi newspaper says will "outdo by far" 9/11, and which will "change the face of world politics and economics," Osama is planning to do "Beslan-style" attacks on our schoolchildren, like the Chechen Muslim radicals did when they took hundreds of students hostage and many were killed or wounded in the school in Beslan, Russia. Our soldiers found maps and diagrams of American elementary schools on the computers of al Qaeda terrorists captured in Iraq. Osama himself has said that what happened in Beslan will happen a thousand times over to American children. And remember one of the earlier fatwas Osama obtained said that 2 million American children must be killed for the sake of parity, and now Osama believes 3 million American children must die (the number was 2 million, but now Osama has raised it to 3 million) saying that 3 million Muslim children have now died as the result of America's aid to Israel, the embargo America put on Saddam Hussein's Iraq, and the casualties caused in the Iraq and Afghanistan Wars. Add to this the disconcerting news that two suspicious Middle Eastern men boarded a Houston area school bus while the children were on it, in a sort of trial run, and also that 14 Houston area school buses have gone missing, probably stolen by terrorists who plan to use them to attack schools. Add to that the news that many of the "Special Interest Aliens," the Middle Eastern Muslim illegals coming across the Mexican border, are swarming into the Houston area. Remember Houston is one of the cities mentioned by 9/11 master planner Khalid Sheik Mohammed (and it was on his laptop computer as well) as being on the target list for Osama bin Laden's "nuclear hellstorm for America," and you have a recipe for disaster!

Chapter Two

One Man's Attempt to Warn America

Having read all five of Paul Williams' brilliant books on Osama bin Laden's plan to destroy 7 to 10 American cities with nuclear bombs, which Osama calls his American Hiroshima plan, and having met in person with Hamid Mir, the courageous journalist who interviewed Osama three times, and having spoken with intelligence experts such as General Tom McInerney, General Paul Vallely, Yossef Bodansky, and many others, and having seen the progression of Osama's nuclear plan, I felt something had to be done to warn America. God has put it on my heart to do everything I can to get this most important subject into the national awareness, and get a full media and government investigation, so that we may stop Osama's coming devastating attack, or at least warn Americans so they will know the right actions to take in the event of a nuclear terrorist strike on multiple cities, and will know how to avoid deadly radiation poisoning, so that millions of lives can be saved.

I have spent $10,000 on an ad in The Weekly Standard, knowing that this important conservative journal is delivered to the doorstep of every Senator and Congressman in Washington, and that it is read by leaders at the Pentagon, the National Intelligence Services, the Supreme Court, and the White House. I spent thousands of dollars on a full page color ad in the Washington Times. I created my first website, www.stopdoomsday.com, which about 20,000 people still visit every year, and I created our new website, www.afcpr.org, the website of our 501(c)(3) non-profit counter-terrorism think tank, the American Foundation for Counter-Terrorism Policy and Research. General Tom McInerney, CNN and Fox News military analyst, is an honorary board member. Dr. Paul Wiliams, former FBI consultant and author of five books on Osama bin Laden, is a board member and Vice President.

I sponsored a debate at The National Press Club that Fred Barnes of Fox News and the Weekly Standard moderated, between Paul Williams and Richard Miniter, about suitcase nukes and Osama bin Laden's plans to use them on America. The debate was on radio and TV, and was covered by such notables as Les Kinsolving, a member of the White House Press Corps, and journalist for World Net Daily.

I personally spoke with, in person, face-to-face, and gave our info to Tom Brokaw, Anderson Cooper, John King, Dana Bash, Wolf Blitzer, Glenn Beck, Catherine Herridge, Sean Hannity, Carl Cameron, Michael Scheuer, Carl Rove, Charles Gibson, George Stephanopoulos, Michael Isakoff, E.J. Dionne and Newt Gingrich. They were all interested, but none so far other than Glenn Beck and Newt Gingrich have done anything to bring this to the awareness of the American people. Shortly after I gave our info to Newt Gingrich, he came out with a major speech saying that America is facing a catastrophe, that a nuclear attack by terrorists is the greatest threat facing Americans, and that our Homeland Security and National Intelligence Agencies are not doing nearly enough to warn and protect the American people.

I also made numerous trips to Congress, to inform and warn our Senators and Congressmen about the enormous threat facing America, the devastating nuclear attack that is coming soon, and to try to get them to hold a Senate and a House Hearing on Osama's American Hiroshima plan, so we can get a full media and government investigation into how far along Osama is in his avowed plan to "kill ten million Americans [three million of them children] with nuclear weapons," as stated in the fatwa he obtained.

I have spoken in person, face-to-face, and given our info to 35 Senators, including Senator Dianne Feinstein, of the Senate Intelligence Committee, Senator Jay Rockefeller, also a leader of the Senate Intelligence Committee, Senator Richard Burr, co-chair of the Senate Caucus on WMD Terrorism, Senator John McCain, Senator Greg Judd, Senator Lindsey Graham, Senator Jim DeMint, Senator John Cornyn, Senator Richard Shelby, Senator Jeff Sessions, Senator Susan Collins, co-chair of the Senate Homeland Security Committee, Senator John Ensign, Senator John Kerry, Senator Dick Lugar, Senator Mel Martinez, Senator David Vitter, and Senator Sam Brownback.

I met with the military legislative fellow for Senator Burr, and Senator Burr's staffer on the Senate Intelligence Committee, and gave them our info, plus Dr. Paul Williams' book, The Day of Islam, and sent them many emails. I met twice with Senator Joe Lieberman's chief of communications, in an attempt to get our info to Senator Lieberman, who is the co-chair of the Senate Homeland Security Committee. Senator Lieberman, to his credit, and Senator Susan Collins, held five Senate Hearings in 2008 on nuclear terrorism, and how un-prepared America is to handle it, hearings which were sparsely attended by the media, which Senator Lieberman was shocked that such an important subject was so ignored by the media (which brings to mind one of Dr. Paul Williams' books, Dunces of Doomsday, which examines the way the media and the government have totally dropped the ball on Osama's coming American Hiroshima attack). I hoped the chief staffer would give our info to Senator Lieberman, indicating that a nuclear terror attack is being planned right now and could occur in the very near future! I hoped Senator Lieberman would hold a Senate Hearing on Osama bin Laden's American Hiroshima plan, so we could get a full investigation of how far along Osama is in his plan to blow up 10 American cities! Although sometimes I wonder if even a Senate Hearing would get the media to cover this most important issue!

In addition to talking to Senators and meeting with their staffers, I also stopped by dozens of Senators' offices, giving our info to other key staffers, and sending emails to just about every Senator's Intelligence and Homeland Security staffers, Republicans and Democrats alike, especially all of the key staffer's on the Senate Caucus for WMD Terrorism, begging them to hold a Senate Hearing on Osama's American Hiroshima plan. In September of 2008 I gave our info to then-Senator Barack Obama, and I was very pleased when, in the second nationally televised TV Presidential Debate with John McCain, Barack Obama said, "We must prevent Osama bin Laden from blowing up American cities with suitcase nukes!"

I also spoke with in person, face-to-face, and gave our info to many Congressmen, and also with their staffers, in an attempt to get a House Hearing on Osama's American Hiroshima plan, in addition to a Senate Hearing. I especially met with staffers of Congressman Jeff Fortenberry, who is co-chair of the House Caucus on Nuclear Terrorism, and I also met with the military legislative fellow for Congressman Mike Rogers of Michigan, who is very concerned about al Qaeda's plans to attack the U.S. I spoke with Congressman Todd Tiahrt of Kansas and he told me he had just gotten an email that Congressman Rogers had sent to all his fellow Congressmen about his concern about the story by Sara Carter in the Washington Times about the al Qaeda leader who was bragging about how a terrorist could easily bring a suitcase full of anthrax into America through the tunnels underneath the Mexican border that the drug smugglers use, which, if properly dispersed in a large city, could kill 300,000 Americans! There is evidence al Qaeda has anthrax and other bio-toxins, in addition to their chemical and nuclear weapons.

I spoke in person, face-to-face, with Congressman Peter King on two occasions, and gave him Dr. William's book <u>The Day of Islam</u> and our other information about Osama bin Laden's plans to do a devastating nuclear, biological, and chemical attack on multiple cities in the U.S. I gave our info to Congressman Peter Hoekstra's main staffer on the House Intelligence Committee, and spoke in person with Congressman Hoekstra. I also gave our info in person, face-to-face, with Congressman Mike Conaway, who is the leader of the House Intelligence Committee.

In addition I gave our info about Osama's attack plans to as many media people as I could, hopefully to get them to do some articles investigating this most important issue – they would not have to say "We think this is going to happen," they could just say "Let's look at the evidence, pro and con, that suggests Osama bin Laden may be far along in his plan for a nuclear attack on America." Wouldn't it have been good if the media had done some investigative work on Osama's plan to crash airplanes into buildings on 9/11? There were many warning signs about 9/11, all ignored by the media. Why was there no report in the American media that Al-Quds Al-Arabi newspaper, a leading Arabic newspaper, published an article by Osama bin laden three weeks before 9/11 saying that he was "going to attack America in an unprecedented way for its support of Israel"? Three weeks later, he attacked America!

Why has there been no reporting in the American media on articles by the London Times, the Arabic newspaper Al-Watan Al-Arabi, and the BBC, reporting on Osama bin Laden's acquisition of nuclear suitcase bombs? Unfortunately, it is the nature of the media to only report about disasters after they happen, instead of investigating potential disasters before they happen, which would give us a chance to possibly prevent the disaster, or at least to warn and prepare Americans to minimize casualties. As has been previously said, after Osama bin Laden's American Hiroshima attack has taken place, and seven to ten, or more, American cities are lying in smoldering, radioactive ruins, what media is left (for much of the mainstream media will be destroyed, headquartered as they are in several of the cities Khalid Sheikh Mohammed has said are targeted by Osama, such as Washington, D.C., New York City, and Los Angeles), what media is left will talk about it endlessly over and over for hours upon hours and days upon days and months upon months, and even for years upon years.

The media, or what is left of the media, will say "Why did we miss this clue?" and "Why did we not see this warning sign, and that warning sign, and this other warning sign?" and "Why did we not examine this, and investigate this, and bring this to the attention to the public?" And "Why didn't we listen to the people who were trying to warn us?"

And the media, what members of the media who have survived the devastation, will certainly ask, "Why didn't our National Intelligence Agencies tell us they were worried about the approaching American Hiroshima Osama was bringing on America?" "Why didn't they tell us the whole truth? Was it because they, as one high level intelligence official told the late Paul Weyrich, founder of the Free Congress Foundation and co-founder of the Heritage Foundation, "We don't want to unduly alarm the public"? Me personally, I'd much rather be warned and "unduly alarmed" about a coming catastrophe so I could prepare for it, than be kept in the dark. Intelligence and Homeland Security officials, and the media, "don't want to scare Americans" we are told, by talking about the possibility, and bringing to light the large body of evidence suggesting a second 9/11 is coming that, according to al Qaeda, is "going to be far bigger than 9/11, and is going to change the political and economic structure of the world!" Me personally, I think Americans need to be scared! We need to be scared into action to stop the attack if we can, and tell people how to avoid deadly radiation sickness if we can't stop it! If a catastrophe is coming my way, I want to know about, don't you?!!! I think the vast majority of Americans would feel the same way.

People naturally ask me, "Dr. Cort, have you told the authorities about this?" Yes, I have told many, many of the authorities about Osama bin Laden's plans for a nuclear attack on the U.S. I met twice with FBI and Homeland Security officials at the FBI office in my hometown of Birmingham. I have written letters about it to FBI Director Robert Mueller and ten other high ranking FBI officials. I have emailed many FBI officials as well. Dr. Williams has met with the highest officials of the FBI. I have met with several mayors of cities in Alabama. I gave our info in person to Douglas Naquin, director of The Open Source Center of the Office of the Director of National Intelligence, who reported three times a week to the Director of the CIA. I gave our info in person to Dr. Mark Lowenthall, who George Tenet had asked right after 9/11 to rejoin the CIA and become the number two man in the CIA. I even gave our info to Fred Barnes of Fox News and the Weekly Standard, who to his great credit took the information to a private meeting with then Vice President Dick Cheney. Perhaps this is why Dick Cheney, to his credit, has over and over again warned that a nuclear and/or biological attack on America by terrorists is coming soon, in one or two years or sooner!

I told the great governor of my home state of Alabama, Governor Bob Riley, about Osama's plans, and Governor Riley, to his credit, arranged a meeting for me with the Director of Homeland Security for Alabama, who I met with and shared our info with for two hours. Then the director of intelligence for the whole Southeast for the Dept. of Homeland Security came over from Atlanta and met with me for two hours. Then, Dr. Paul Williams, who as I mentioned before in the Introduction to this book, is the genius who first brought Hamid Mir's warnings that Osama had acquired nuclear weapons to light, and who is "the Sherlock Holmes" of this thing (with me being essentially the humble Dr. Watson), and who is on the board of our counter-terrorism research foundation, the American Foundation for Counter-Terrorism Policy and Research (please see our website www.afcpr.org for more info), and who has written five landmark, blockbuster books on Osama bin Laden's American Hiroshima plan–Dr. Paul Williams, and I, were asked to come to Washington D.C. to meet with the Senior Director for Combating Terrorism of the National Security Council, and the Director for Combating Terrorism of the National Security Council, at their offices in the White House Compound!

It was a beautiful sunny day in Washington as Dr. Paul Williams, Jeff Bell, who helped arrange the meeting, and I walked to the White House Compound for our meeting with the Senior Director and the Director for Combating Terrorism of the National Security Council. Jeff, a consummate Washington insider, had helped arrange the meeting. We had originally thought the meeting was going to be in the West Wing itself, for the business cards of the Directors clearly had "The White House" printed as the address. However when we were checked through security at the gates of the White House Compound, which includes the White House, the West Wing, and the Eisenhower Executive Office Building, the guards took us to the Eisenhower Executive Office Building, just across a narrow alley from the West Wing. Later that evening, when I had a tour of the West Wing, I saw why the meeting was held in the Eisenhower Building – the West Wing is actually very small, and the Situation Room is smaller yet. The Eisenhower Office Building, by comparison, has many offices of Intelligence and National Security, and it is where most business is conducted on Security issues.

I was very glad to see the inside of the Eisenhower Executive Office Building, for it was in these very halls that my grandfather, General Hugh Cort, (I am Hugh Cort, III) walked when the building was first built. My grandfather was studying pre-med at Johns Hopkins and was on track to go to medical school when World War I broke out. He joined the army as a private, and loved the life of a warrior so much he made a career of it, and advanced through the ranks to become a General in World War II. While most generals came out of West Point, my grandfather did it the hard way, coming up through the ranks, from private to general. He was buddies with Patton and McArthur, and is the only man known to ever make George Patton quit cussing, if only temporarily! When my grandfather (who we called "Chief," because in 1943 he was Chief of Staff of the U.S. Army VII Corps) was stationed in Hawaii in the late 1920's, he was a lieutenant, and George Patton was a major.

Back in the twenties, the army was still making the transition from horses to mechanized vehicles. A lot of army bases had horses, in addition to motorized vehicles. And those bases had polo teams. Major George Patton was the captain of the polo team, and my grandfather was one of his best polo players. They were playing against an opposing team in a heated match one day, and Patton was cussing a blue streak, as was his custom. My grandfather, who was a preacher's kid, objected to the steady stream of profanity, and he said, "Major Patton, if you continue to use profanity, I will be compelled to quit this team on the spot!" Patton, after hearing this, looked like he had swallowed a grapefruit, and turned several shades of purple. Knowing he would lose the polo match if my grandfather, their best player, were to quit, Patton finally spit out the words, "All right, Cort!" and did not curse the entire rest of the match! However, as we all know, that cessation of profanity from George Patton was only a very temporary thing!

My grandfather was asked by General Omar Bradley to assist General Plank as Quartermaster to get all the equipment ready for the D-Day Invasion of Normandy, because they knew Chief was somebody who could "Get things done" and who could be counted on to get the Allied troops ready for D-Day. My grandfather, who had the heart of a warrior, as does his son, my father, Hugh Cort, Jr. (who was in World War II and also in Korea, where he was a tank commander wounded in battle and nearly killed many times), objected to being in charge of Quartermaster work, because he was a combat soldier and he only wanted to be in combat. But General Omar Bradley convinced him the Allies needed someone who could get the job done right. So Chief took the assignment, with the understanding that he would be allowed to get back into combat as soon as D-Day was completed, and not be doing Quartermaster work.

Chief took on his assignment with his usual dedication and tenacity, and only slept 4 hours per night in the months before D-Day, getting the tanks and guns and ammo all ready for the big invasion. He did take an afternoon off to attend a reception with the King and Queen of England at Buckingham Palace that the Royal Couple gave for the American Generals and their staffs in appreciation of their saving England from the jaws of defeat by the Nazis. Later, during the months of preparation in England to get the D-Day Force ready for the coming Normandy Invasion, Chief was invited, along with General Woodruff, to dine with the King and Queen on two occasions. He wrote a letter home mentioning how the Queen was very gracious, and when she spoke with you, she focused entirely on you, as if you were the only person in the room.

As soon as D-Day was accomplished, my grandfather got his wish to get out of Quartermaster work and back into the frontlines of combat. He was asked to lead troops in the Pacific, where he fought in 22 island invasions, as the Allies made their way from the Philippines to Japan itself. My buddy General Tom McInerney told me when he and my other friend General Paul Vallely were young cadets at West Point (General McInerney went through West Point before becoming a Lieutenant General in the Air Force), they studied my grandfather's excellent preparatory Quartermaster work for the D-Day Invasion, which is taught at West Point as an example of how to prepare for battle. I'm bragging here, I know, about my grandpa, but I am very proud of him and my very brave father also!

Getting back to me and Dr. Williams and Jeff Bell, as we climbed the many steps up to the impressive entrance to the Eisenhower Executive Office Building, I felt an awe as I walked the same halls my grandfather walked, when, just after World War II, he was on the Joint Chiefs of Staff, and also on the National Security Council, and was the liaison between the two! Which brings to mind one last important story my grandfather told me, about his days working with President Truman during the Korean War. When General Douglas McArthur wanted to have the Air Force destroy the Chinese Army, which had come into North Korea across the Yalu River, which our Air Force could have easily done, President Truman held a meeting of the National Security Council, which my grandfather was a member of, to decide what to do. My grandfather told us that at the meeting was a member of the Treasury Department's Intelligence branch. This man told the group that he had information that if America destroyed China's Army, Russia was going to enter the war on the side of China, and it was going to become World War III.

President Truman and the members of the National Security Council did not want another World War, so they denied McArthur's request to destroy the Chinese Army, and as a result, instead of being able to hold the entire nation of Korea like McArthur wisely wanted to do, our troops were driven back and we had to settle for a tie, so to speak, with South Korea being free, and North Korea being under Communist dictator control. And now we are facing today great danger as the rogue state of North Korea is sending its nuclear technology, and probably someday soon even a nuclear bomb, to other rogue nations like

Iran, Syria, and Myanmar, and possibly even to terrorist groups, not to mention actively threatening our cities on the West Coast of America with nuclear ballistic missiles! And now let us hear, as Paul Harvey used to say, "the rest of the story!" The Treasury Department Intelligence official who said Russia would enter the war if we destroyed the Chinese army, my grandfather told me, died a year or two later. He lived alone and did not have any next of kin, so Security Council staff were asked to clear the things out of his apartment. When they got his things, they were shocked to find all kinds of documents showing that he was a spy for Russia, a mole planted in the National Security Council, and that Russia had had no intention whatsoever of entering the Korean War on the side of China, but Russia had asked him to pretend to the National Security Council that Russia was going to enter the War, in an attempt to bluff the United States and their allies into thinking Russia was going to enter the war. Unfortunately, their bluff was successful, and paid off! My grandfather later told me that goes to show how crucial it is to have good and correct intelligence, and how devastating it can be when you have faulty intelligence.

Our meeting with the Senior Director for Combating Terrorism, and his second in command, the Director for Combating Terrorism lasted almost two hours, and they listened to us very carefully. We gave them lots of our information brochures, and also gave them Dr. Williams' classic textbook about Osama's American Hiroshima plan, The Day of Islam: The Annihilation of America and the Western World.

They gave me their email addresses, so I periodically send them updates on any new information we get. Yes, some people may say, "How can you, Dr. Cort and Dr. Williams, presume to know something our Intelligence Agencies don't know, and you are giving them info? Don't they know the info already?" Again, as I explained in the Introduction to this book, USA Today newspaper had on its front cover, and CNN had a feature story, on how 90% of the information the FBI and CIA and our other National Intelligence Agencies (there are 16 agencies in all) get, anyone can get from what is called "open source" information on the internet and elsewhere, as opposed to classified info. In fact, the USA Today article and the CNN story emphasized that our National Intelligence Agencies should really be focusing more on open source info, like terrorist jihadi websites on the internet (we have several sources who can translate from the Arabic), and spend less time waiting for dribbles of classified intelligence from informants who may be incorrect, or even making up things in order to get paid for their intelligence, and they are missing some vital things on open source. And you would be amazed at how much our Intelligence Agencies don't know! For example, the FBI did not even interview Hamid Mir, the Pakistani journalist who interviewed Osama bin Laden three times, who found out Osama had acquired suitcase nuclear bombs, until Hamid went to them later on! You would think the FBI would be interested in talking to a man (Hamid Mir) who had interviewed Osama three times, and who is the only man who interviewed Osama after 9/11! Our Intelligence Agencies let us down big time on 9/11, and they are going to let us down on the next 9/11, Osama's American Hiroshima attack. Our government, and our National Intelligence Agencies, and our media, need to do their job, and tell the American people that Osama is definitely planning this thing, and give us the information they have so far, and tell us what to do in the event, God forbid, of a nuclear attack by terrorists on our cities, which could possibly occur by the end of this year, or sooner! Is that too much to ask?

Chapter Three

Cort for President! – The Presidential Run to Warn the Country: How It All Started

Having tried every way possible to alert the country to the impending nuclear threat from Osama bin Laden, al Qaeda, and Iran, the coming American Hiroshima, I decided to turn my hand to politics, in the hope of getting some media investigation of the coming attack. I first ran for office in the 2006 Alabama Republican primary election for state representative, hoping to perhaps get elected as state representative in the Alabama House of Representatives, my home state, my thinking being that if I were elected as state representative, I could later possibly be elected to Congress, where I could have some influence on counter-terrorism issues facing the country, and, most importantly, where I could give speeches in Congress that C-SPAN would cover, that could break the media strangle-hold on the American Hiroshima story. You know, when, God forbid, Osama does blow up ten American cities, and nuclear mushroom clouds are rising above them, we will forever wonder why the media choked off every story, every investigation, every mention of Osama's American Hiroshima plan. Here was the greatest danger to ever face America, and the media was afraid to touch it with a ten foot pole. As a psychiatrist, I often see patients using the psychological defense mechanism of denial to avoid dealing with disturbing and upsetting facts, but the denial seen in our media is truly astounding. Like ostriches fervently burying their heads in the sand to avoid seeing approaching danger, as if this would make it go away, the media steadfastly refuses to see or investigate the many blatant clues that Osama is planning and is very close to executing his evil Grand Finale, his life's work, his American Hiroshima. There are so many more clues of Osama's deadly intent for his coming attack than we ever had about 9/11, yet the media will not discuss a one of them. The negligence, lack of investigative courage and curiosity, and downright malpractice of the media, in failing to warn us of the coming disaster, will be a topic of discussion for years, decades, and even for centuries to come!

Three alternative media sources, however, must be mentioned and commended for their great work in trying to get the vital story of Osama's coming American Hiroshima attack out to the public and into the mainstream media. These are the genius work of Dr. Paul Williams in the five blockbuster books he has written on the story, the many, many articles on the subject by Joseph Farah, editor of World Net Daily, the popular internet news site, and the fearless, intrepid journalistic investigative work of the courageous Pakistani journalist Hamid Mir, who has risked his life countless times to interview Osama bin laden and Taliban and al Qaeda mujahideen. Martin Mawyer, of Christian Action Network, who, expanding on the original work done by Paul Williams, has brought to light the paramilitary training camps of Jamaat-ul-Fuqra that are training terrorists right here in America! And Yossef Bodansky, the former Director of the Congressional Task Force on Counter-Terrorism for 16 years, is to be commended for his excellent book <u>Chechen Jihad</u>, which describes in detail how Chechen Muslim rebels stole 20 suitcase nuclear bombs from the former Soviet Union and sold them to Osama, who then hired several former SPESNAZ Soviet Special Forces soldiers whose job it had been to service and maintain the suitcase nukes for the KGB, to maintain the nukes for Osama. Dr. Paul Williams' five books on Osama's American Hiroshima plan, <u>Al Qaeda, Brotherhood of Terror</u>, <u>Osama's Revenge: The Next 9/11 --What the Media and the Government Haven't Told You</u>, <u>The Al Qaeda Connection: International Terrorism, Organized Crime, and the Coming Apocalypse</u>, <u>The Dunces of Doomsday: 10 Blunders That Gave Rise to Radical Islam, Terrorist Regimes, and the threat of an American Hiroshima</u> (our media is definitely one of the Dunces of Doomsday!), and his newest book, <u>The Day of Islam: The Annihilation of America and the Western World</u>, will be read and re-read for centuries, as the definitive books that outlined in extensive, exhausting detail, the huge volume of evidence indicating that Osama bin Laden was going to devastate America with nuclear attacks. Paul Williams will be forever known as the Paul Revere who tried to warn America "The Nukes are coming!"

So, to try to get some media coverage of Osama's American Hiroshima plan, I decided to run for President of the United States! I ran in the 2008 Republican Primary race against John McCain, Mike Huckabee, Duncan Hunter, Ron Paul, and the rest. I had at first planned only to get on the ballot in New Hampshire, and campaign in New Hampshire for a few weeks before the Republican Primary in January of 2008, in hopes of getting Osama's American Hiroshima plan mentioned in a few New Hampshire newspapers. It only costs $1,000 to get on the ballot in New Hampshire, and no petitions with signatures are required. And the New Hampshire Secretary of State, Bill Gardner, is famous for his welcoming and acceptance of all bona fide candidates for President. Bill feels strongly that all Presidential candidates, even the lesser known candidates, should have a chance to present their views to the American people, and Bill goes to great lengths to give the Lesser Known Candidates, as he graciously calls us, the opportunity to be heard, even inviting us to participate in a Presidential Debate on C-SPAN, which is broadcast not only in the U.S. but around the world!

In January of 2007, I, with the help of my computer-genius friend, Patrick Gallivan of Contrive Media, a web-site design and software company, designed a great website, CortforPresident.com, where my views and info about Osama bin Laden's coming attack, the American Hiroshima, were posted. You can still see my 2008 Campaign Website if you Google "Hugh Cort" and click on the first entry, "Dr. Hugh Cort for President." To my surprise, I soon got a call from Steve Kush, of Kush and Associates, an election campaign PR company. Steve has managed political campaigns for Senators and Congressmen, and had even run the Presidential campaign of John Cox, an Illinois Republican who was the head of the Cook County Republicans, a very large, million member-strong organizations in Chicago. Steve had succeeded in getting John Cox on the front page of the Los Angeles Times, and had gotten John a lot of good speaking engagements. John and Steve had a falling out, and Steve had come across my website, and was very impressed that I was trying to stop the next 9/11!

Steve, like myself and all Americans, was shocked and horrified by 9/11, and wanted to do whatever he could to prevent another terror attack by al Qaeda on America. Steve had an especially close connection to 9/11. On the morning of 9/11, Steve was working in his office in Jersey City, just across the Hudson River from Manhattan. Suddenly, one of his staff called to him and said, "Steve, You gotta come outside! An airplane has just hit one of the World Trade Towers, and the Tower is on fire!" Steve went outside, and he and his staff watched the Tower burn. Then, to their surprise, they heard a horrible screaming roar and looked downriver to see the second hijacked jetliner flying low above the Hudson River, and watched in horror as it crashed into the second World Trade Center Tower! Then for five days afterward, Steve helped dazed survivors as they walked through the Holland Tunnel from Manhattan, and helped get them medical treatment and shelter. Being a very patriotic American, and having served in the United States Marine Corps, Steve decided then and there to do everything in his power to prevent another 9/11 from ever happening again.

So Steve offered to be my Presidential campaign manager, for half the price he usually charges, to get our message out to America. And boy did we get our message out! We estimate we reached 30 million Americans through radio, TV, newspaper, and internet coverage of our campaign! We got on the ballot in six states, and were in caucuses in three states. Our TV campaign commercial aired on Fox News and CNN in six states. And we were on the local TV affiliates of ABC, NBC, CBS and Fox all across Iowa, South Carolina, New Hampshire and many other states.

I hired Steve February 5, 2007, and he immediately got to work getting me registered as a Presidential Candidate with the Federal Elections Commission (FEC), and assembling a team of volunteers around the country. Jack Stiles, the co-director of the Christian Coalition of Virginia, proved to be a stalwart, dedicated, and hard-working volunteer, and later paid staffer, our Campaign Chairman for the great state of Virginia. Jack got on the phones, and soon had lined up, with Steve's help, my first political speaking engagement, at the Republican county breakfast in Virginia Beach, Virginia.

I flew up to Norfolk, took a cab to Regent University in Virginia Beach, televangelist Pat Robertson's Christian University, where Nancy Shuman met me to show me around the University. Nancy is a brilliant Christian conservative pro-life activist, who took an interest in my campaign. Nancy, who was completing her degree at Regent University, took me to see Dr. Charles Dunn, Professor and Chairman of the School of Government, a close friend of Pat Robertson. I was very keen to get our information to Dr. Dunn, as I hoped he would get it to Pat, and perhaps Pat might take an interest in my Pro-Life, Get America Back to God, stop Osama's American Hiroshima, Presidential Campaign. One of the main reasons I was running, in addition to warning people about Osama's coming attack, was to be a "voice crying in the wilderness" like John the Baptist, to warn people that America has gotten so far away from God, what with abortion and homosexual marriage, that we have gotten away from God's protection, His "umbrella of protection" as it were, and that terrible things are going to happen a million times worse than 9/11!

Let us take a close look at the travesty of abortion. Over 50 million unborn babies have been slaughtered since Roe vs. Wade became law in 1973. If you will google "Silent Scream" you will see the video of the ultrasound of an actual abortion done in the 80's. The ultrasound is grainy, since in the 80's that is the way ultrasounds were when the technology was first developed. The ultrasound shows the 11 week old fetus (at two and a half months approximately when women first discover they are pregnant, and about the earliest they get an abortion). The fetus swims in fear to the very back of the womb in a futile attempt to get away from the forceps of the abortionist. When the abortionist's forceps rip off its arms and legs, the fetus opens its mouth wide in a giant scream, a scream no one can hear because the fetus is in the womb, hence the term "Silent Scream."

The abortionist who took the ultrasound was Dr. Bernard Nathanson, who had done 10,000 abortions. He had always wondered what actually happened during an abortion, what the response of the fetus might be, and now that ultrasound technology had improved, he had the ultrasound done at the same time he was performing the abortion (now the most widely done operation in the United States). When he saw the helpless fetus open its mouth wide in the Silent Scream, he exclaimed in horror, "Oh no, they do feel the pain! He quit being an abortion doctor on the spot, and became a Pro-Life activist!!!

There was a bogus "study" done by some researchers with heavy ties to the abortion industry (yes, it is an industry – they make huge amounts of money doing over a million abortions a year), which said that fetuses don't feel pain until about 7 months or so. This is an out and out lie. I personally took care of prematurely born babies in the prenatal intensive care unit at Cooper Green charity hospital in Birmingham when I was doing my Pediatrics rotation in medical school, and part of my job was to stick the 6 month old infants in the heel to draw blood for blood tests to monitor kidney function, etc. And let me tell you, anyone who has done a heel-stick on a 6 month old infant will tell you they definitely feel the pain!

At a lecture during the Ob/Gyn rotation in medical school at the University of Alabama at Birmingham (UAB), Dr. Michael Flowers, then head of the Ob/Gyn Department, gave us some news that shocked me to the core. As best I can remember his words, Dr. Flowers said, "Medical students, I am in favor of abortion. However, I must tell you something. The media is always talking about how many times an abortion has to be done to 'save the life of the mother'. But you, as physicians, need to know the truth about this. There is never a time when an abortion is necessary to save the life of the mother." I was completely shocked, because I had heard so often even dedicated Pro-Life conservative Republicans, repeat the mantra that they are against abortion "except in the case when it is necessary to save the life of the mother, or in the case of rape or incest." So to find out that the prevailing belief, held by all of America, that abortion is sometimes necessary for the life of the mother, is totally wrong, was a real shocker to me.

Dr. Flowers went on to say that even if a woman is in a coma, it is actually medically safer to wait and deliver the baby at term than to do an abortion. It used to be that a mother with certain rare types of advanced cervical cancer was thought to be at risk if they deliver their child, but now that is no longer the case. And there is one life-threatening complication of very high blood pressure, called Pre-eclampsia, which almost always occurs at 5 or 6 months or more into the pregnancy, where the baby has to be delivered, so that the mother's blood pressure can return to normal. But even in that rare situation, the Ob/Gyn doctors do not do an abortion, which actually takes three days, with all the preparatory steps. No, they have to get the high blood pressure situation resolved immediately, to save the life of the mother, and to do so they go ahead and deliver the baby. And notice, I did say deliver the baby, and not kill, or abort the baby! Then they put the baby in the prenatal intensive care unit, and the babies 6 months or more usually survive and thrive. And even the few 5 month old babies are put in the prenatal unit, and given care, and if they die they die a natural death, and not a cruel inhumane death by the body part amputation or saline poisoning of abortion. And abortion has a number of medical risks, including death. Also, many young girls who get abortions find themselves sterile and never able to have a baby later on. There is an increased incidence of breast cancer among women who have had an abortion. And the emotional trauma can be devastating. As a psychiatrist, I can tell you many women who have had abortions feel guilt and grieving for years after the event, and have only found peace and forgiveness after accepting Jesus as their Savior, and accepting His forgiveness.

I would also like to debunk the idea that abortion is okay in the case of rape or incest. I was blessed to be able to go to an event that was held as part of the 2004 Republican

Convention in New York City. I was a little late for the luncheon, and I hurriedly entered the room and quickly sat down at the nearest table, where people were already eating lunch. I happened to look at the person sitting to the left of me, and to my surprise it was none other than the keynote speaker, televangelist James Roberson, who proved to be a very kind, friendly, and cordial lunch buddy! But I was even more surprised when he got up to give his speech and said, "I am here to tell you today that I am the product of rape!" You could have heard a pin drop. "My mother," he continued, "was raped. Everyone was telling her, 'You need to abort your baby'. But my mother said, 'I believe God wants me to have this baby, He doesn't want me to kill it, and I am going to have this baby and I am going to dedicate it to God'. And she gave birth to me, and dedicated me to God, and let me tell you, I am so glad she did not abort me, and I'm so glad to have life and be here with you today!"

So here is James Roberson, one of the greatest evangelists of all time. a man who God has used in a great and mighty way to save the souls of thousands of Africans and Americans, and to save the lives of thousands of African children through his food ministry in Africa! Just think of the loss to the world if he had been aborted! This goes to show that every life is important, even the life of a child of rape, and that every child, even a child born through rape or incest, if dedicated to God can, through God's grace and power, do mighty works that help hundreds and thousands of fellow travelers on this earth.

There is never a time, not ever, when abortion is necessary for the life of the mother, or needed to kill a child born of rape or incest. We conservatives need to stop accepting the lie and the platitude that abortion is wrong "except in rape, incest, or for the life of the mother." Abortion is wrong in each and every situation. Abortion is murder and it is never, ever justified! Evil liberals (yes, I say evil, because no matter how well-meaning they are, no matter how nice and kind and good to neighbors, no matter how much charity work they may do, anyone who is in favor of tearing the arms and legs and heads off of innocent unborn children, who, as former abortionist Dr. Bernard Nathanson said "DO FEEL THE PAIN," is definitely evil) will use the excuse to give abortions to millions of women for "their health" or " save their life." The old adage that once the camel gets his nose in the tent, the next thing you know he is all the way in the tent with you, is true in the case of allowing abortion "for the life of the mother [which we now know is not true], for rape, or for incest." Once you allow abortion, the abortion industry will use any excuse to continue to do millions of abortions.

A lot of good Christian conservatives are happily living under the delusion that since President Bush and Congress voted to stop partial birth abortion, one of the most barbaric and cruel forms of infanticide ever practiced in the history of man, that evil practice was indeed stopped. But guess what? Thanks to a liberal judge in, you guessed it, California, the Act of Congress has been stayed, until eventually it works its way up to the Supreme Court, and in the meantime thousands of babies are getting their brains sucked out by vacuum pumps as the horrible practice continues. And another terrible thing about it is that these partial birth abortions are done primarily for the convenience of the abortionist, since they are easier to do than the regular abortions, where the abortionist is required by law to count and document all the pieces after the abortion, to make sure he got both of the arms, both of the legs, the head, and the torso, because even if only one piece is accidentally left in the mother, the mother will get a bad, possibly fatal infection.

For those of you that don't know, partial birth abortion, of which about 5,000 are done every year in the United States, is the procedure where a 6 to 9 month old baby, who could easily survive if born (we have six month old "preemies," prematurely born babies who survive and thrive all the time in the prenatal care units), are pulled out of the mother's birth canal by the feet until the baby is all the way out except for the head, which remains stuck in the birth canal because it is too big to come out. In natural birth, the mother goes through hours of labor, which gradually expands the birth canal so the baby's head can come out. To solve the problem of the baby's head being too big to get out of the birth canal, the partial birth abortionist takes his closed scissors and stabs the baby in the base of the back of the neck, opening a hole where the spinal cord comes into the brain, so that he can then insert a vacuum tube which sucks the baby's brains out, down the tube, and into a container, thus conveniently collapsing the skull so that now, Voila!, the baby's head can now come out of the mother, and now the baby can be delivered, now dead. How satisfying it must be for the abortionist, delivering a dead baby, which he has freshly killed! A nurse who participated in a partial birth procedure said that when the abortionist plunged his scissors into the back of the baby's neck, the baby flung out its arms and legs in a spasm of agony--remember, this barbaric procedure is done without any anesthesia whatsoever, on 6 and 7 and 8 and even 9 month old babies that most certainly feel the horrible pain just like you or I would! And yes, I call them babies, and not by the potentially dehumanizing term fetuses, because the 6-9 month old babies killed in partial birth abortions could survive and live as babies if delivered, and in the case of younger than 6 months, even though of course the technical term would be fetus, anyone who has seen an ultrasound, and watched a fetus suck its thumb and stretch and yawn, knows this is a live human being, an unborn baby waiting for its chance to enter the world.

Whether it's by partial birth abortion at 6 months or more, or regular abortion at 2 to 6 months, where the arms and legs and head are pulled off by the abortionist's forceps, or whether it's by saline abortions, which are not done very much anymore, where the baby poisoned by the saline, would you like this to happen to you? Why don't they do an ultrasound of an abortion now, since today we have very advanced ultrasound that could show us in vivid detail what happens during an abortion? Because the media knows if the American people saw what actually happened in an abortion they would be horrified, and they would vote overwhelmingly for a Constitutional Amendment banning abortion forever! I mean, how would you like to have your arms and legs pulled off? Can you believe America is doing this to over a million unborn babies a year?!!! Our Founding Fathers would turn over in their graves if they knew American mothers were violating the civil rights of their own children, paying an abortionist to kill their own child. What ever happened to our God-given right to life, liberty, and the pursuit of happiness?

A mother's womb ought to be the safest place in the world for a baby--but for over a million babies a year, it is the worst place to be, where their own mothers ask an <u>abortionist</u> (not a doctor, because a <u>true</u> doctor would never do such a thing) to rip their arms and legs off with a forceps and then count the pieces afterward to make sure all the limbs are out. Even the first primitive doctors in ancient Greece knew abortion was wrong. In the Hippocratic Oath, which every doctor takes when graduating from medical school, it clearly states, "Neither will I administer a poison for anybody when asked to do so, nor will I suggest such a course [euthanasia, or assisted suicide]. Similarly I will not give a woman a pressary to cause abortion." So why are we violating the Hippocratic Oath and killing thousands of unborn babies every <u>day</u>? And why are we killing our elderly with euthanasia in Oregon? In Holland, where euthanasia is wide-spread, thousands of elderly are killed every year <u>without their consent</u> so that their adult children are spared the cost and hassle of caring for them, and so the children can inherit their money sooner. Adult children, killing their parents! What is next? Are we going to be like the Nazis who killed over 200,000 handicapped people because they were a burden to the state?

It is not enough to just overturn Roe vs. Wade. Although this would be a good first step, all it would do would turn the abortion decision over to the states. So you would have some states allowing abortion and some states not allowing abortion, just like in pre-Civil War days you had some states allowing slavery and some states not allowing slavery. If some states are doing abortions, you still have a nation that is killing unborn babies, committing grievous sin in the eyes of God. Why are we killing our babies, when there are couples waiting in line to adopt babies, and even going to foreign countries and paying thousands of dollars to adopt babies? For every couple that adopts a baby, there are a thousand on the waiting list that want to adopt a baby. But there aren't enough babies here in America to adopt because we are aborting them! Sav-A-Life and Lifeline and other Christian organizations regularly help thousands of pregnant women financially and medically for 9 months and even longer to have their babies, and then either keep the baby or give it up for adoption to a good home. Why don't we do this with all of our unborn children whose mothers are not ready for motherhood? There are plenty of want-to-be mothers who will be glad to adopt. Why are we embracing a culture of death, instead of a culture of life?

If America stops killing unborn children, and turns away from its many other sins, and turns back to God, God will again bless America. But if America persists in abortion, and its other evils, we will be away from God's protection, and plague after plague, and disaster after disaster, will come upon America, until finally we are destroyed, and the "Shining light upon a hill" will be extinguished. If you go to the Jefferson Memorial in Washington, D.C. you will see, inscribed on the walls surrounding the statue of the great man, words that say, "Indeed I tremble for my country when I reflect that God is just, that His justice cannot sleep forever." Jefferson was talking about God's judgment that would come upon America in the Civil War for the abominable sin of slavery. These words can now also describe God's judgment that is coming on America for the abominable sin of abortion. Jefferson also said "God who gave us life gave us liberty. Can the liberties of a nation be secure when we have removed a conviction that these liberties are the gift of God?" If the Supreme Court ever rules that we must drop the words "one nation, under God" from the Pledge of Allegiance, it will be another sign of the beginning of the end of America.

Another major sin that America is committing against God is the legalization of homosexual marriage. As much as we like to rationalize, and no matter how fair and reasonable it seems, to call the homosexual relationship "marriage" is crossing a line of blasphemy that has never been crossed before in history, until recently. Not even Sodom and Gomorrah had the nerve to call the homosexual relationship "marriage," yet they were wiped off the face of the earth. I believe that we should treat homosexuals with dignity and compassion, as Jesus would have us treat all people. But conferring God's Holy Sacrament of marriage on the homosexual relationship, which in the Bible God does not approve of, is slapping God in the face, and will bring about a judgment far worse than what happened to Sodom and Gomorrah. Every civilization that has embraced homosexuality has "gone down the tubes" and disintegrated. The same fate awaits America, if we do not change course.

Chapter Four

The Presidential Run, Continued – Virginia, Iowa, and South Carolina

So, thanks to Nancy Shuman, I was able to give our info about Osama's nuclear attack plan to Dr. Charles Dunn, Dean of the School of Government at Pat Robertson's Regent University in Virginia Beach, Virginia. Dr. Dunn was very kind and helpful, and listened with interest to our latest information. I hope he passed it along to Pat and Gordon Robertson, so they could see the latest info we have. My friend, colleague, and mentor, Dr. Paul Williams, had met with Pat Robertson for over two hours in the past and explained to Pat how Osama bin Laden was planning multiple nuclear attacks on American cities. That is why Pat said in his annual New Year's predictions that terrorists were going to kill millions of Americans in nuclear attacks in the near future! Dr. Paul Williams also influenced Pastor John Hagee through his writings, and the writings of Ryan Mauro, who has done great work in following up on Paul Williams' work by interviewing Hamid Mir again. That interview, on Osama's nuclear arsenal, can be seen in the Appendix of this book. Pastor John Hagee quoted Dr. Williams and Ryan Mauro for 2 pages in his great book <u>Jerusalem Countdown</u> in Chapter Two, titled "An American Hiroshima?" Dr. Charles Dunn was kind enough to give me a copy of his book, <u>The Seven Laws of Presidential Leadership</u>.

The next morning I met with the Virginia Beach Republicans Club for breakfast, for my first speech on the campaign trail, other than my speech on Jan. 21, 2005 announcing my run for the Presidency in the Zenger Room of the National Press Club, the day after George Bush was inaugurated for his second term, and one speech I had done previously at the Vets Vision/ Circle of Friends for American Veterans center in Arlington, Virginia, where I spoke right after Douglas Feith, who was number three man in the Pentagon at the time. When I gave my press conference Jan. 21, 2005 at the National Press Club, I was at that time just planning to get on the ballot in New Hampshire and my home state of Alabama. But of course Steve Kush, my national campaign manager, changed all that when we went nation-wide in Feb. 2007. But getting back to my speech at the National Press Club, the day before my speech, I was waiting for the Inaugural Parade for George Bush to start. I was in the bleachers with my colleagues from the President's Club of the RNC, right next to the bleachers with the Washington Press Corps. It was freezing cold, and the only warm hat I could find in the hotel gift shop was a tall, Cat-in-the-Hat type of hat, with red, white, and blue stripes, very patriotic, if a bit humorous in its outsized way, an "Uncle Sam hat," I call it. I was really a little embarrassed about it, and I was actually looking for a garbage can to throw it away, but it was so cold I decided I had to keep it, or else my ears would freeze! Well, no sooner had I put it on, than a lady from CBS asked me if I could do an interview. I said "Sure!" and the next thing I knew, there I was being interviewed live on national TV by Russ Mitchell, reporting back to Dan Rather in the studio.

Russ asked me what I thought about George Bush's Inaugural Speech, and I said it sounded very good, and then Russ asked me about my own Presidential ambitions, because I had told him about my plans to enter the 2008 Republican Primary. So I was able to invite the entire country to my press conference the next day at the National Press Club announcing my candidacy for President of the United States! Let me clearly say I did not enter the race, being a lesser known candidate, thinking I could win. I got into the race to bring media attention to, and to warn the American people, about the great danger facing America. At the end of the interview, Russ Mitchell, in his final words, said to Dan Rather, "Well, there you have it, Dan! The first candidate to declare in the 2008 Presidential Race!" And Dan Rather, on national TV, said, "I'll take your word for it, Russ!"

Flash forward to February, 2007, as I am about to give my first speech actually on the 2008 campaign trail (since the first Republican primaries were due to take place in January and February of 2008, it was imperative to begin active campaigning a year ahead). I read a speech Steve Kush had prepared for me, and then spoke some other words as well. Then we quickly bundled into the cars and took off on a snowy day for a trip across the entire length of the state of Virginia, to give a speech that evening in a town right at the border of Virginia and Kentucky. The snow got heavier and heavier, and soon we were creeping along, carefully navigating a frozen stretch of highway where eight to ten cars and trucks had already slid off the highway into the valley of the median, stranded! We were running late, but we called ahead and told the event organizers to hold on, we were coming as fast as we could! Somehow, we made it to the town, but then got lost trying to find the meeting place of the County Republicans, as snow fell more and more heavily. Finally we made it to the event, where just about the whole crowd had waited for us to arrive. I gave my speech, again reading from the speech Steve had written for me, which did a good job outlining my views, and then I ad-libbed and added some more info. Also we gave out plenty of campaign material, and the information we had about Osama's American Hiroshima plan. The people were very interested and grateful we had come that long distance to see them.

After my speech, as we wound down back at the hotel, my stalwart Virginia campaign chairman, Jack Stiles, gave me some very important advice--he said, "Doc, drop the written speech, and speak from your heart." Over Steve Kush's objections, I did just that, and felt so much better speaking my own words from my heart, without a script or teleprompter, or anything. And this shall I always do, if I ever run for office again!

The next morning, the President of the County Republicans invited us to her church. We were enjoying the service, when to my surprise the pastor invited me up to the pulpit to say some words to the congregation. I said, "I am running for President to stop abortion and homosexual marriage, and get America back to God, so that we get back under His protection, or else I fear a million times worse than 9/11 will come upon us." To my further surprise, I got a huge ovation, Praise the Lord! But none of these pleasant surprises could match the final surprise, when we got back in the cars and were leaving, when Steve Kush said to me, "Doc, did you realize you were just now on TV, and you were seen by thousands of people in 7 states?" I was totally shocked! I did not realize the church was televising the service, and had a very large multiple state viewing audience! For a political nobody like me, to be able to get my vital message out to thousands of people, was quite a thrill! And now I knew why Steve Kush, political genius that he was, had had us drive seven hours through the snow across the entire state of Virginia, because he knew we were going to get this great television exposure. It was only the first of many great adventures we had across the country, where Steve Kush was able to get such a totally unknown political novice as myself into the media spotlight to get our vital warning out to America! Of course, in addition to Steve Kush's hard work and political genius, I knew we had the great power of the Lord behind us, as we took His message to the American people, and, as it would prove later, even to our brothers and sisters "across the pond" in England!

Our next campaign adventure was the Lincoln Dinner in Des Moines, Iowa. Just about all the Republican candidates were going to speak, including John Cox, who was a lesser known candidate, just like me, having never served in political office. Steve Kush had arranged for me to be a speaker also, we thought, with the same officers of the Iowa Republican Party who had arranged for John Cox to speak. I was very happy about this, because the speeches were to be on C-SPAN. Finally, I would accomplish my heart-felt goal to get Dr. Paul Williams' and my warning out to the media and the American people that Osama bin Laden was planning a nuclear strike on America. At the event I got to give a brochure with our info, and briefly explain it, to all the candidates: John McCain, Rudi Giuliani, Mike Huckabee, Tom Tancredo, Duncan Hunter, Jim Gilmore (the former Governor of Virginia), and Tommy Thompson, with the exception of Ron Paul, who did not attend; Fred Thompson, who would enter the race later, when I did get to give him our info (who then later, to his great credit, brought to national attention for an all-too-brief moment, the threat that suitcase nukes in the hands of Osama bin Laden pose to America); and Mitt Romney, who I was not able to speak with, but whose wife and son I was able to talk to later on in the campaign.

All of us candidates had a room provided where we had our campaign literature, and I had copies of my book to give to folks, <u>Saddam's Attacks on America: 1993, September 11, 2001, and the Anthrax Attacks</u>, published in 2004. After 9/11, 70% of Americans had a gut feeling that Saddam Hussein had had a hand in the 9/11 attacks, and, although the media continually suppresses any mention of it, the truth is that Saddam was very angry at America for kicking him out of Kuwait, and he assisted Osama bin Laden's attack on America. There were deep, decade long ties between Saddam Hussein and Osama bin Laden and al Qaeda, as evidenced in Stephen Hayes' great book, <u>The Connection,</u> about the ten year connection between Saddam and Osama. For example, did you know that Osama bin Laden met in Baghdad with Tariq Aziz, Deputy Prime Minister? And Ayman al-Zawahiri, the number two man in al Qaeda, met in Baghdad with the Vice President of Iraq? And on and on and on! The first chapter of <u>The Connection</u> is titled "Who was Ahmed Shakir?" Stephen Hayes writes that Ahmed Shakir was an Iraqi intelligence agent who was observed by Malasian Intelligence when he flew from Iraq to Kaula Lumpur, where he met two of the soon to be 9/11 hijackers at the airport and took them to a three day planning conference with Ramzi Binalshibh, the "paymaster for 9/11." After the conference, Ahmed Shakir, the Iraqi intelligence agent, took all the participants back to the airport, and they all flew home to their respective countries and Ahmed Shakir flew back to Iraq. The FBI later called this meeting in Kuala Lumpur, "the pivotal planning session for 9/11." So here we have an Iraqi Intelligence agent facilitating the "pivotal planning session" for 9/11! The media ignored and supressed this information, because it was their conscious or sub-conscious plan to dump on President Bush and make him look bad for invading Iraq, so that they could elect a Democrat President in 2008, which they succeeded in doing! So the media did not want to report on any news that showed that Saddam did have a hand in 9/11, and President Bush was correct in invading Iraq. The media did the same thing with the WMD thing.

Saddam's General of the Air Force, Georges Sada wrote a book you can get at Barnes and Noble or Amazon.com titled <u>Saddam's Secrets</u>. In his book, General Sada describes how a month before the Iraq War, Saddam ordered him to take a Boeing 747 and five Boeing 727's and strip out all the passenger seats, and load them to the gills with chemical and biological WMD, and the planes made 56 round trips to Syria the month before the war! And General Sada reports there were numerous convoys of eighteen–wheeler trucks on the ground below hauling tons of chemical and biological WMD into Syria the month before the war. I myself have seen Israeli Intelligence photos of those convoys! So there were WMD, weapons of mass destruction, but Saddam transported them to Syria the month before the war!

Former CIA Director James Woolsey testified that he believed Saddam had a hand in 9/11, especially in training the terrorists how to hijack airliners at Saddam's terrorist training camp at Salman Pak, near Baghdad, and Laurie Mylroie, who has taught at Harvard and the U.S. Naval War College, wrote how Saddam assisted Osama in the 9/11 attacks in her book, <u>The War Against America-Saddam Hussein and the World Trade Center Attack-A Study of Revenge</u>.

At the Lincoln Day Dinner in Iowa, however, I learned a tough lesson in the land of politics. Even though Steve had paid five thousand dollars (of my own money!) to the same organizers who charged the same thing to get lesser known candidate John Cox on the speaker list for the event, and he had the same agreement, when the event came about I was not called to speak! I later found out that the two organizers did me wrong, and had not even mentioned me to Ray Hoffman, the Chairman of the Republican Party of Iowa. Those two organizers have now been replaced, I might add. When Ray found out I had been excluded, he was very sorry about it, and immediately invited me to go with him and Senator Sam Brownback on his upcoming cross-country Chairman's Tour of Iowa, where we would give speeches across the state. He asked me to invite my good friend General Tom McInerney, who I had met at some counter-terrorism conventions (General McInerney and General Paul Vallely, another friend of mine, wrote the highly acclaimed book <u>Endgame: The Blueprint for Victory in the War on Terror</u>), to come with us also and speak about the growing threat of Iran getting nuclear weapons and how to stop them.

Needless to say, I was very very disappointed I did not get a chance to speak on C-SPAN with the other candidates at the Lincoln Dinner in Des Moines, Iowa in April of 2007, the first really big event of the 2008 Republican Primary race. For the first time I realized this was going to be a much different Primary than the Bush, McCain, Alan Keyes, Gary Bauer, Steve Forbes Primary of 2000, where candidates like Keyes, Bauer, and Forbes who had never held elected political office were able to be in the televised national debates along with Senator McCain and then-Governor Bush, the only truly viable candidates in the race. In that 2000 Republican Primary, the two main contenders, McCain and Bush, needed other warm bodies out there on the debate platform to make it look like a real debate, and not just a two-horse race, even though in actual fact it was essentially a two-horse race. This is not to disparage the good contributions to the political discourse of the nation that truly brilliant debaters like Alan Keyes brought to the table. In fact, in several of the debates, Keyes was acknowledged as the clear winner! But in the cold, hard realities of politics, it is not always the best ideas or the best debater that wins the election, but at least the idealist "lesser known candidates" got to speak their piece and get their views heard by America, which is all I wanted to do. In fact, I felt strongly, and still do, that my information that Osama bin Laden is planning a nuclear attack in the near future on America is the most important topic facing the country, even if I was the least important person to bring it up!

However, I soon realized that this 2008 Republican Primary was far, far different from the Primary of 2000! There were more than plenty of warm bodies to fill the debate stage, and all of them had solid credentials and could have been elected President. Every one of the main contenders were Senators, Governors, or Congressmen, and lesser known idealistic candidates were going to have a very hard time being heard, even if their message, as in my case, was absolutely the most essential, crucial, life-saving message America needed to hear. So I was very disappointed to spend all that money and fly Steve and our staffer Rich Holt and myself all the way out to Iowa, and not even get a chance to speak, especially where I was hoping to break my important info on C-SPAN, the biggest news story in the history of America, that Osama bin Laden has acquired functional nuclear weapons, has probably already smuggled them into our country, and is just waiting for the right galvanizing moment in history (probably the point when Israel attacks Iran's nuclear facilities, coming soon) to pull the trigger and devastate ten American cities in nuclear blasts, accompanied by biological anthrax attacks, chemical attacks, and armed assaults Mumbai-style by thousands of well-armed al Qaeda and Hezbollah and Jamaat-ul-Fuqra militiamen!

Even though I was deeply disappointed I didn't get my vital message to the nation on C-SPAN that day in Des Moines, several good things came out of our trip to the Lincoln Dinner. We met lots of patriotic Iowans, and gave them our campaign literature and counter-terrorism info, and copies of my first book, Saddam's Attacks on America, and I got to meet and make friends with a lot of political king-makers in Iowa politics, such as Ray Hoffman, the Chairman of the Iowa Republican Party, who is a really great guy, Darrell Kearney, the Treasurer of the Republican Party of Iowa (RPI), as the party is formally known, Big Leon Mosley, a truly great man in heart as well as size, Steve Scheffler, the President of the influential Iowa Christian Alliance, and Gopal Krishna, the treasurer of the ICA, valiant Steve Rathje, Republican Senatorial candidate, and lots of other Iowa politicos. And I got to give my counter-terrorism info to McCain and Giuliani and Tancredo and Duncan Hunter and all the big candidates, to make them aware of it. And I got to dance to the song "Sweet Home Alabama" played by none other than Mike Huckabee and his band at the reception!

And you know, sometimes defeat can inspire us to greater efforts to succeed. I was so mad and disappointed at not getting to speak, that when I got home I looked up the next event coming up on the campaign calendar, and I saw an event in a suburb of Columbia, South Carolina, which was going to be held by the Lexington County Republicans. I said to Steve Kush, "Steve, let's go to this event, and please make sure I will get to speak at the event!" So off we went to South Carolina, another of the key campaign states, being one of the first three states in the nation to hold their Primary election, along with Iowa and New Hampshire. We arrived in the lovely Palmetto State, and I immediately felt right at home, in a conservative Southern state very similar to Georgia, where I spent my teenage years, and Sweet Home Alabama, where I have been very happily living for decades. It was a beautiful sunny morning the day of the event. Steve had secured my speaking spot with an email confirmation from one of the event organizers, and we were good to go!

I stood by the door and greeted every one of the three hundred or so people as they entered the event, warmly shaking their hand, welcoming them to the event, and giving them each my campaign brochure (you can see a copy of it in the appendix to this book), with the words, "Hey there, I'm Dr. Hugh Cort, the Pro-Life, Pro-Marriage Presidential Candidate, and I'll be one of the speakers here today." The people were genuinely interested in my campaign brochure, which really resonated with their good down-home Southern values of the importance of family, sanctity of life, and God. And they were interested in our counter-terrorism info! Most Americans know in their hearts that Osama bin Laden is not finished with America. In fact, 66 % of Americans believe that Osama will strike America again, and this time it will be a nuclear attack. And they are right! If only our "lamestream" media would do its job and investigate the biggest attack on America ever planned, coming soon to a neighborhood near you!

First the Governor of South Carolina, Governor Sanford, addressed the crowd. Then Senator Lindsey Graham spoke to the crowd, and then Senator Jim DeMint spoke. Several representatives of Presidential candidates spoke, and then I got a chance to speak, and then after me the Attorney General of South Carolina spoke. Evidently the crowd liked my campaign brochure which I had personally handed out to each person as they entered the door, with our platform of Christian conservative values, and our plan to stop abortion and gay marriage and get America back to God and His protection, stop Osama bin Laden's coming attack on the U.S., secure our borders and stop illegal immigration, and win the War in Iraq by sending in another 100,000 troops (eventually the "Surge" did send in 30,000 extra troops, greatly stabilizing Iraq, showing that our plan was a good one), and our plan to stop Iran from getting nuclear weapons, and our plan to win the War on Terror. How did I know the crowd liked our campaign brochure? They gave me a huge ovation as I was going up to the podium, before I even started to speak! I'm telling you, people like our values, which are the same values that cause conservative crowds to go wild when Sarah Palin speaks! Folks are hungry for a leader who believes in their good old common sense Christian conservative values! After my animated speech, I got another huge round of applause! Thank you, good people of South Carolina! After my speech I gave our counter-terrorism info to Senator Graham and Senator DeMint, who were very interested in it.

I was to speak many more times in the great state of South Carolina before the Primary election in January 2008. I got to speak another time at an event along with Governor Mark Sanford (whose political star unfortunately has dimmed recently, but who was high in the polls back then). I was very tired after a number of campaign trips around the country in quick succession, and I was looking forward to spending a week at home with my wonderful wife Debbie, when Steve Kush called me and said, "Doc, we have to go to South Carolina. I know you need a rest, but we gotta go – it is a real important event." I reluctantly agreed to hit the campaign trail again so soon after other events. Duty calls! Sure enough, Steve was right on the money – this was a very big event! In Spartanburg, my trusty South Carolina Campaign Chairman, Dean Allen, met me and Steve and soon was introducing us to the dignitaries, who included Governor Sanford and the South Carolina Secretary of State. Then Governor Sanford addressed the crowd, and then I spoke, and then the Secretary of State spoke. I got a very big ovation from the crowd. They were shocked to hear that Osama bin Laden was much farther along in his plan to do a nuclear attack on America than anyone had thought. And they liked my Christian conservative platform! A retired General in the audience later told Steve after my speech, "I agreed with every single thing that man said!"

At another event near Aiken, South Carolina, where my wife and I had often visited my mother-in-law when she was living in the Aiken area, I got to speak at a large event of over 500 South Carolina Republicans along with Katon Dawson, the Chairman of the South Carolina Republican Party, and the South Carolina Secretary of State. Katon came up to me before the speeches, and thanked me for paying $35,000 to the Republican Party of South Carolina to get on the ballot (all the other candidates only had to pay $25,000, except me and Fred Thompson, who had to pay extra because we filed late, after the deadline – I filed late because I had not been sure if I wanted to get on the ballot, it being so expensive, as compared to New Hampshire, which was $1,000, or Alabama, which was $5,000, or Texas, $4,000, or Missouri, $5,000, or Iowa, which was free, being a caucus state, or Rhode Island, and the other states where I got on the ballot. But as time went on, even though I knew I did not have a chance to win, I felt I needed to be on the ballot in South Carolina, one of the first three primary states, in order to really make a run of it and get my vital message out to America. So I grudgingly coughed up $35,000 of my own money to get on the Primary ballot in South Carolina (I got very little campaign dollars in contributions – people liked my views but understandably were reluctant to contribute money to a lesser known candidate with little chance to win). Katon Dawson told me right before I went up to speak that the famous comedian, Stephen Colbert, had wanted to get on the South Carolina ballot, but balked at paying the $35,000 entry fee. He asked Katon if he would waive the fee or give him a discount, but Katon told him, "No, Mr. Colbert, you have to pay the $35,000 just like Dr. Hugh Cort did!"

Many people have asked me why I spent all my money on a campaign that had little or no chance to win. I tell them I did not run to win, I ran to get the message out to America that a devastating nuclear attack from al Qaeda, assisted by Iran, is soon to come upon America. I guess it is my strong protective instinct, my sense of wanting to protect the people of America from the disaster that is heading toward them. If you knew what I knew, and what Paul Williams knows, and what Hamid Mir knows, (and I have tried to convey that knowledge to you, so that you will know too), you would, like me, be doing everything in your power to try to warn everyone and stop this terrible nuclear Holocaust that is coming soon to America! I am reminded of the Revolutionary War Patriots, many of whom were merchants whose entire wealth was their ships, who gladly sank their own ships in Boston Harbor to clog up the channel to prevent the British Navy from entering the harbor, which ensured victory for George Washington's troops that day. Or the owner of a beautiful mansion overlooking the harbor, who, when he saw the British had commandeered his mansion and were using it as headquarters for their assault on Washington's troops, showed no hesitation when he told General Washington to aim the cannons right at his mansion, and blow it to smithereens!

By paying the fee to get on the ballot, I was qualified to speak at the Christian conservative Family Values Debate in South Carolina where all the other candidates either spoke in person or spoke via videophone. I got my points across, and got some votes in the Straw Poll held after the debate, but I did not sway the crowd with a charismatic speech the way Steve Kush, Jack Stiles, Dean Allen, and my other State of South Carolina Campaign co-Chairman George Mabry had wanted. But I learned a good lesson. The speech, and the speaking style, are very very important. For example, how did Barack Obama beat the hugely experienced political machine of Hillary and Bill Clinton? It was Obama's charismatic, stirring speeches, plus his community organizing skills at winning the caucuses (with ACORN's help), plus his enchantment of the press, which was eager for a fresh new face, and which recognized in Obama an ultra-liberal who would implement all their far left liberal schemes, and who would be much more pliable than the Bilary team (Bill and Hillary). But it was Obama's oratorical flair that really got things going for him – as Steve Kush put it, "The speech is the thing!." In retrospect, I realize I was giving the audience a lot of very good and important ideas, especially our plan to save America from nuclear destruction, but I was doing it in a rote, overly serious, machine gun-like way, trying to cram too many facts and concepts into the limited 7-10, or at the most 14 minutes allotted for a speech at nearly all of the campaign events. The times I did the best was when I had an hour to speak, when I had plenty of time to cover all the issues, and relax and take my time, and not be rushed.

Such a time was my hour long speech and question and answer session with the Iowa Christian Alliance, a copy of which you can see in the appendix of this book. I had to pay the Iowa Christian Alliance $5,000, which was their standard fee for addressing their group, which several other candidates paid as well to address the group. I felt it was worth the money, because the money was going to a good cause (the Alliance does good work to elect Christian conservatives, although they made a big mistake in not supporting Steve Rathje in his bid to be the Republican Senatorial candidate to face Democrat Senator Tom Harkin in the November election). The ICA also put my speech on their state-wide website, which was very influential. I felt my strong stand on not just overturning Roe vs. Wade, but stopping abortion nation-wide with a Constitutional Amendment, plus my stand on affirming the traditional marriage of a man to a woman with the Federal Marriage Act, and get America back to God and His protection, and stopping a nuclear American Hiroshima attack by Osama bin Laden, plus our plan to win the War in Iraq by sending in 100,000 more troops, and our plan to stop Iran from getting nuclear weapons, would resonate with the good Christian people of Iowa. I gave a nice, relaxed speech, in a friendly, down-home conversational style, because I had plenty of time, and a good question and answer session where the folks got to ask about their concerns. At the end of the speech, our photographer in Iowa, free-lancer Allison Joyce, even though she had a lot of liberal views, being from New York, said, "Dr. Cort, you really rocked!" Steve Kush said "Doc, if you can speak like that every time, you can be President some day!" So if I ever run for any political office again, I will not try to cram too many facts in, and speak in a machine-gun, New York minute fashion. I'll just get a few major points in, in a relaxed, friendly conversational way, and I'll connect with the crowd much much better!

One of my favorite Iowa events was the two day, cross-Iowa Chairman's Tour of Iowa, with Ray Hoffman, the Chairman of the Republican Party of Iowa, Darrell Kearney, the Treasurer of the RPI, Senator Sam Brownback, and my good friend, General Tom McInerney, where we traveled across Iowa giving speeches in Sioux City, Des Moines, and Cedar Rapids. Ray Hoffman and Darrell Kearney had asked me if my friend General Tom McInerney, noted military analyst for CNN and Fox News, would go on Ray's Chairman's Tour of Iowa and give speeches along with Ray, and some of us Republican Presidential candidates. Ray is very concerned about Homeland Security, the threat of Iran getting nuclear weapons, and other counter-terrorism issues, and he admired General McInerney's strong stand on defending America, and stopping Iran from getting nuclear weapons and giving them to terrorists. I asked General McInerney if he would be interested, and put him in touch with Ray and Darrell. To all our delight, the valiant warrior agreed to accompany us!

Our first stop was Sioux City, Ray's home town. Ray gave a speech, then General Mac, then Senator Sam Brownback, then me, then John Cox, and then Daniel Gilbert, another lesser known, but very idealistic, candidate. We all got a good response from the crowd, especially General McInerney, as you might imagine. All four local TV affiliates, ABC, CBC, NBC, and Fox covered the event, as did several Iowa newspapers and radio stations. Then we all headed for Des Moines to a barbecue with the Des Moines Republicans, where we had a good time cooking burgers for the people, and, you guessed it, giving speeches! Again we had good TV and newspaper coverage. The next day we all headed to the eastern part of the state to Cedar Rapids, where we again gave speeches. At the end of my speech, I got ovations on all five of my main campaign questions – 1. Do you want to stop abortion and homosexual marriage and get America back to God? 2. Do you want to win the War in Iraq? 3. Do you want to stop Iran from getting nuclear weapons and starting a nuclear World War III where 200 million people will die? 4. Do you want to stop Osama bin Laden's coming nuclear attack on America? and 5. Do you want to win the War on Terror? Or, as many would say, the War Against Islamic Fascism!

We went on many other campaign trips in the great state of Iowa. I enjoyed telling the Iowa crowds, "I have more roots in Iowa than any of the other candidates. My great-grandfather was a circuit-riding preacher in Iowa, my grandfather taught military science at Iowa State before he became a General in World War II, and my Dad played football for the Little Cyclones of Ames High! When you vote for me, it's practically like voting for an Iowan, although one with a Southern accent!" We were greatly helped by our Iowa campaign staff: Pastor Patrick Anderson, and his lovely family, Steve Huff, and John Utz. One fascinating event was the Iowa Straw Poll, a big national event with all the major candidates. Although I had declined to pay the $50,000 fee to be a speaker at the event, I did get a booth, and we gave our info to a lot of voters and media people, and we also had a counter-terrorism convention the night before the Straw Poll. Every campaign traditionally has some kind of event the night before the Straw Poll, and we put on a big event at a local hotel with none other than Dr. Paul Williams, who really discovered the fact that Osama bin Laden is not only planning a devastating nuclear attack on multiple American cities, but that he is very far along in his preparations, and the attack is coming soon! Paul Williams and his wife Pat flew all the way out to Iowa to join us. At the counter-terrorism convention, Paul and I spoke at length about Osama's American Hiroshima Plan. You can see the videos, and our 2008 campaign website, with many of the speeches I gave, by googling Hugh Cort and then clicking on the first entry, "Dr. Hugh Cort for President." There you can also see our dynamite TV campaign ad that we ran on CNN and Fox News in six states, by clicking on "View Hugh Cort Campaign Commercial." Ray Hoffman was one of the people who attended Paul Williams' and my speeches, and he received an autographed copy of one of Paul's books.

The next day dawned bright and sunny and hot! The Iowa Straw Poll! Our trusty group hiked about half a mile through the crowded parking lot to the grounds of the Straw Poll, where we set up our booth on the crowded fairway. Our campaign staffers included Rich Holt, Dean Allen, Jack Stiles (a true political junkie if I ever did see one!), our photographer Allison, Kathryn, our college intern who was doing a political science internship with our campaign, and of course the unstoppable man of political action, Steve Kush, and yours truly, Dr. Hugh Cort, counter-terrorism expert and Republican candidate for President of the United States of America! (Boy, that has a great ring to it, doesn't it!). We gave out tons of my books, and campaign literature, and counter-terrorism info. I was interviewed by several foreign media reporters, including ones from Germany, Australia, and the Netherlands, all of whom were very interested in Osama's American Hiroshima plan. It was hot as blazes, and we were covered with sweat ,but we got our message out, and we had a great time. There was a humorous incident that happened right as I was leaving the Straw Poll to go home to my sweet wife Debbie, who had been ill a few days before the Straw Poll, and I could not wait to get home to be with her. I was hurrying, getting ready to leave our booth to head to my rental car, when a kindly old man, casually dressed in jeans and a plaid shirt, came up and said "Hello, Dr. Cort! I'm a Presidential candidate, too!" I looked at the elderly gentleman and thought to myself, "Here's some nice old guy, another lesser known candidate, who has even less of a chance to win the Presidency than I, bless his heart!" I could tell he wanted to talk, but I was in a big hurry to catch my plane, so I said to him, "It's nice to meet you, Sir, but I've got to run catch a plane, cause my wife has been ill and I've got to get home to her," and I hurried away. The gentleman had never given me his name, and I wondered who he was, and what his particular campaign issues might be.

About a week later, I happened to be watching TV and I saw a news clip, and there was the gentleman – to my shock, I realized it was Ron Paul!!! I fortunately did get a chance to meet him again several times on the campaign trail, and we did get to talk!

One of the most memorable Iowa campaign trips was the night of the Iowa Caucus, where the eyes of the entire nation were turned to Iowa to see the results of the very first Primary Election in the nation! I had the privilege, thanks to my good buddy Leon Mosley, who strongly felt that every candidate, whether famous or not, had a right to speak, to be one of the Presidential candidates to address the 5,000 person crowd at the Caucus in Waterloo, along with Mike Huckabee, who ended up winning Iowa that night, and Ron Paul. Ron Paul spoke first to the crowd, then Mike Huckabee spoke, then I spoke. I'm telling you, the crowd listened more intently to me than they did to Mike Huckabee, as I told them about Osama bin Laden's plans for a nuclear attack on America! A hush came over the crowd when I told them Khalid Sheikh Mohammed, Osama's main planner for 9/11, had told the CIA and the Pakistani Intelligence when he was captured, and it was on his laptop computer as well, so we know it wasn't just waterboarded out of him, that "Osama bin Laden is planning a nuclear hellstorm for America, and he has targeted ten cities: New York, Washington, Philadelphia, Boston, Miami, Chicago, Houston, Los Angeles, Las Vegas, and Valdez, Alaska, site of the biggest oil terminal in the U.S."

Steve and I pulled out of the packed parking lot after the event, got some food at a restaurant, and headed back to Des Moines, where we only had a few hours to sleep until getting an early flight to New Hampshire, where we had a Veterans' event where ABC <u>National</u> News was going to do a special news report on the lesser known candidates and film my speech. It was late at night, and as we drove across the frozen Iowa landscape, after about 45 minutes of driving on the Interstate, I had a funny feeling that we were perhaps going the wrong way. We usually got a GPS with our rental cars, but the press had already snapped up all the rental cars with a GPS, so we didn't have one on this trip. I said, "Steve, do you think we may be heading east, instead of west? Steve said, "Uh-oh." When we came to the next roadsign for the next exit, and looked at the map, sure enough, it turned out we had just spent 45 minutes driving the wrong direction! So we turned around about 1:30 AM, and retraced our way back to Waterloo, and then continued on the long journey back to Des Moines. I got to bed about 4 AM, and we had to get up at 6 AM in order to catch the only flight available to New Hampshire (again, the press had snapped up most of the flights).

Fortunately I was used to functioning with little or no sleep during my medical school and residency days! New Hampshire, here we come!

Chapter Five

The Presidential Run, Continued: New Hampshire

After getting about two hours sleep the night of the Iowa Caucus, Steve and I flew onward to New Hampshire. After changing planes, our second flight took us into the Manchester airport about 5:30 PM, where we met the rest of our trusty campaign crew who had earlier flown into Manchester – Dean Allen, Jack Stiles, George Mabry, and also Dan Herren, who, like Steve Kush, had been with the John Cox campaign before signing on with us. It was quite an expense to fly everyone up to New Hampshire (remember, I did all of this on my own money, since, being a lesser known candidate, we got very little in the way of campaign contributions, although if, God forbid, Osama bin Laden does blow up ten American cities I'm sure folks will wish they might have helped us get our message out, especially the slackers in the media). But even though it was expensive, I wanted to give the guys a real live campaign experience, like we had at the Iowa Straw Poll, and campaigning in New Hampshire on the eve of the New Hampshire Presidential Primary Election was really something!

At the airport, we were met by our New Hampshire Campaign Chairman, the hard-working, dedicated Chris Richter, a fine young Christian conservative, who has written some really great conservative articles, and who, like the rest of us, was a rock-solid Pro-Life, Pro-Marriage, Pro-America, Pro-God Christian conservative trying to save America. I can't say enough good things about my wonderful campaign staff. They worked for our campaign for a fraction of what they could have made with other campaigns, because they, like me, fear that America is going to be attacked in the near future by Osama bin Laden, assisted by Iran, and they are great Patriots who want to do everything they can to prevent another 9/11. So Chris and Steve and Dan and Dean and Jack and George and I piled into the cars and immediately headed for the Veteran's Vision/Circle of Friends for American Veterans event that my terrific friend, Major Brian Hampton, was holding in a suburb of Manchester.

Brian was the one who had arranged for me to speak in Arlington along with Douglas Feith, then the number three man in the Pentagon (by the way, the Feith Memo definitely did show that Saddam Hussein and Osama bin Laden and al Qaeda had huge, decade-long ties with each other, as you can see in Stephen Hayes' book <u>The Connection,</u> about the ten-year connection between Saddam and Osama). Brian held rallies all across America in the early Primary states and elsewhere, promoting the cause of Veterans' rights and getting shelter for homeless veterans (Circle of Friends for American Veterans sponsors 17 shelters for homeless vets, and Veterans Vision is the name of their magazine). Brian was kind enough to invite me to speak at a number of their rallies, where I spoke along with young Beau Biden, Vice-President Biden's son, Senator Jim Talent from Missouri, who is now the Co–Chairman of Congress' Commission on the Prevention of Weapons of Mass Destruction Proliferation and Terrorism, and many other notables. Brian was also the one who videotaped my announcement speech for my Presidential run at The National Press Club that cold but sunny day in Washington January 21, 2005. Brian has done so much for our nation's veterans, and he surely has done a lot to help me get my vital warning out to America!

So we were heading for Brian's big Veterans event in Manchester, and I was excited, despite my exhaustion from our Iowa Caucus trip. The amazing Steve Kush had really got something going here, because he had talked ABC National News into covering my speech that night at the Veterans event! ABC was doing a special on the Lesser Known Candidates, as some of us were known, and they were going to put me on national news! I was very excited because now I would finally accomplish my fervent goal of getting the info about Osama bin Laden's coming American Hiroshima attack out into the media and the public's awareness. The whole reason for my campaign, to warn America about the coming devastion of a nuclear attack on multiple cities by al Qaeda, assisted by Iran, was finally going to happen!!!

But there was a problem...like the Iowa Caucus, all the rental cars with GPS direction systems (Tom-Toms) had been snapped up by the media, and our rental car, and Chris Richter's car, did not have a GPS! It was a dark night, difficult to see street signs, and none of us knew how to get to the event, and we only had a half hour before the event, with ABC News in attendance, would start! We prayed, and God answered our prayer! Chris Richter used his blackberry to punch in the address, and the mini-GPS system on it guided us to the event, where we were just in time. We heard that Democrat Presidential Candidate Bill Richardson had come a few minutes earlier, but when he heard the ABC film crew was there to interview me, and not him, he left!

The ABC News crew was very nice, and they followed me all around as I spoke with veterans and explained our findings that Osama bin Laden had acquired suitcase nuclear bombs and had a plan to blow up ten American cities. Then it was time for me to give my speech, and I was happy to see the ABC cameraman filming my speech! Finally, I would break the story of Osama's American Hiroshima attack plan on the National News, and I would get my warning out to America! However, when the TV Special was run a few days later, on the eve of the big ABC Democrat and Republican Debates, instead of my interview and speech, ABC ended up showing a clip of Albert Howard, another one of the Lesser Known Candidates, instead of me! I was so disappointed.

I think the real reason ABC nixed my interview was they were afraid to bring up Osama bin Laden's American Hiroshima plan on national TV, because they were afraid they might "alarm Americans." Hey folks, if I'm about to get blown up by a nuclear bomb, I would like to get "alarmed," wouldn't you?!!! I am always amazed at the way the media has ignored the "elephant in the room," and gone out of its way time and time again to avoid talking about Osama bin Laden's avowed plan to kill ten million Americans! Is it because 93% of the media vote Democrat, and they don't want to bring up terrorism because they know when Americans get worried about terrorism they turn to the Republicans to protect them, knowing the Democrats are always weak on defense and Homeland Security? Or is it they are so afraid to go away from the herd of the rest of the media and explore a topic the others are afraid to touch, for fear they will be called alarmists, or whackos? To do the story, they wouldn't have to say "This is true, or this is going to happen." They could simply say, "Here are some researchers (Paul Williams, Hamid Mir, Yossef Bodansky, and Dr. Hugh Cort) who say Osama bin Laden may have functional suitcase nuclear bombs, and may be much farther along in his avowed plan to blow up ten American cities than has been previously thought."

Now I know what many of you are thinking – you're saying, "But this would cause a mass panic!!!" But which is worse – to tell people the scary truth, and cause them to panic, and also motivate them to try to prevent this coming attack, or at least prepare for it (millions of Americans could be saved from deadly radiation poisoning if they are simply warned to stay in their homes for three days after the blast, and then they can go outside for a ten minute trip once a day, and after two weeks they can go outside all the time), or to not tell the people, give them no warning, and not only see millions of people die in the ten nuclear blasts, but see millions more die from radiation as they rush to their childrens' schools to get their kids, only to learn later, as they and their children sicken and finally die an agonizing death a month later from that brief exposure to deadly radiation, that their kids should have stayed inside at school and the parents should have stayed inside at home or work for three days, and then they could have taken the short trip to school and back to bring their kids home. Remember, many more people died from radiation in Hiroshima than died in the initial blast.

And our schools should be prepared for this. Each school should have a plan to keep the kids inside for at least three days, and have enough food and water on hand to do that. And each school should have on hand potassium iodide pills for the kids, who are at a huge risk to get thyroid cancer from the radioactive iodine produced by the blast, like thousands of children and adults got in Chernobyl. Just one potassium iodide pill a day for several days is all that is needed to prevent thyroid cancer! But no, we don't want to prepare schools, because we "don't want to alarm people and cause a panic." Folks, we need to alarm people and cause a panic, if need be, although I really don't think the American people would freak out and panic, I think they are tougher than that, and I think they would simply take it to heart, and work diligently to investigate Osama's American Hiroshima plan, and try to stop it, or at least prepare for how to survive it. After all, Americans didn't panic when President Eisenhower told them to prepare for the possibility of a nuclear attack by the Soviet Union, that had thousands of nuclear missiles aimed at the United States. No, people simply got prepared, and went about their business. In fact, if God forbid Osama does succeed in blowing up ten cities, and accomplish his stated goal of killing ten million Americans, three million of them children, I think the surviving Americans are going to very angry at the media and the government for not warning them!

So why has the media and the government been so closed-mouth, so reluctant to even broach the subject of Osama's American Hiroshima plan? Do they think if they just ignore it it will go away? Are they like Neville Chamberlain, in total psychological denial of the danger, naively hoping for "Peace in our time" and failing to deal with the immense threat that is facing us? I think it goes much deeper, to basic spiritual warfare. Saint Paul tells us in the New Testament "we are not battling against flesh and blood, but against principalities in high places." The war is between the spiritual forces of good versus the forces of evil. America has gotten so far away from God's wisdom and protection, what with abortion, gay marriage, and the attitudes and beliefs that go along with those two travesties, that, like the sinful Israelites that had turned away from God and got carried off in chains into slavery in Babylon, "their hearts were hardened, and their ears could not hear, and their eyes could not see" the guidance of the Lord. America has gotten too close to Satan, and fallen into his clutches. There is a spiritual freeze, a paralysis that Satan has put on America. Satan has blinded America to what is about to happen, and America has let him do it!

Some people have asked me, "God is a loving God. He won't allow ten million Americans to be killed in nuclear attacks by al Qaeda." My response to that is Yes, God is a loving God. But when a nation gets away from God, it also gets away from God's guidance and protection. God gives us freedom to either choose His ways or reject them, and He gives nations freedom to follow His ways, or reject them. And when a nation turns away from God and His guidance, that nation often fails to do those things that are necessary for survival, and that nation fails to take the right measures necessary to prevent terror attacks. Why did God allow the Nazis and their allies to bring World War II upon the world, where 62 million people died? God had given freedom for the nations of the world, and some nations (Germany, Italy, and Japan) chose to do evil, and other nations (England and the United States) failed to take action to stop Hitler when he was small, and gave him time to develop his war machine, and then it was a million times harder to stop him. Why did God allow 9/11 to happen? Again, I think America had gotten away from God and His protection, and America failed to do the things necessary to stop Osama's ongoing War against America. America ignored all the warning signs: the first attack on the World Trade Center in 1993, the bombings of the U.S. embassies in Kenya and Tanzania, and the attack on the U.S.S. Cole. And now we are stubbornly ignoring all the warning signs of the coming American Hiroshima, even though those signs are way bigger and more numerous than the warning signs for the first 9/11. Wake up, America, before it's too late!

Getting back to New Hampshire, we had a lot of fun campaigning and giving speeches at a lot of places in New Hampshire. We had a very enjoyable time meeting the Secretary of State of New Hampshire, the kind and affable Bill Gardner, who had the Associated Press interview us when we formally got on the ballot in New Hampshire, at the State Capitol in Concord, which is a beautiful Capitol, if a small one, reminiscent of the Talladega County Courthouse back home in Alabama near where my parents lived. I got to sign my name and put a comment on the giant blow-up of the New Hampshire voters notice that all the Presidential candidates, both Democrat and Republican, signed. It was fun seeing my signature and comment right by that of Hilary Clinton, John McCain, and Mike Huckabee! My comment was "God bless you, God bless America, and America bless God!"

Bill Gardner also invited us to participate in the C-SPAN televised debate of the Lesser Known Presidential Candidates. The afternoon of the debate found us about an hour's drive away from the debate site in Manchester, where I was getting a haircut by a barber in Concord who traditionally cuts the hair of all the Presidential Primary candidates, if they will make a donation to the Autism Foundation (the barber's son has autism, and he has done a lot to raise money for autism research), The amazing Steve Kush had arranged for two reporters from Time Online, the online edition of Time Magazine, to interview me and take pictures of me getting the traditional Presidential Primary haircut! It really was amazing how Steve Kush got me so many great interviews and choice speaking engagements, especially with me being a total political unknown. Steve tried to get his friend at C-SPAN who did the C-SPAN Campaign Trail series on a lot of the candidates at Town Halls to do one on me, and although we came close, we never got to do a Town Hall on C-SPAN, which was a shame. God forbid, if Osama does blow up ten American cities, we'll all wish I had been on C-SPAN and gotten the warning out to America!

But we did get on C-SPAN for the Lesser Known Candidates Debate, which was great. We almost didn't make it to the debate, though, because as my New Hampshire Campaign Chairman, Chris Richter, and I got out of the barber shop in Concord, snow had started to pour down, and we did not know if we would be able to make it to Manchester in time for the debate. As we crawled along at a snail's pace in a long line of cars carefully navigating the snow covered road, and as more snow poured down on us, I prayed to the Lord for Him to somehow get us to the debate on time. Chris was an expert at driving on the snow, being a New Hampshire native, and he skillfully got us to the debate site, the TV studios of the Public TV station in Manchester. We hurried inside, the TV cameraman put the microphone on my lapel, and I joined the other candidates for what would be a very spirited debate. I had no idea at the time that not only were Americans watching the debate on C-SPAN, but "across the pond" in England several young Oxford University students were watching as well--Josh Roche, the President of the Oxford Union, the prestigious Oxford debating society known around the world, Charlie Holt, the president-elect (he was to be the president the next year), and the beautiful Emily Gardner, a longtime member and supporter of the Oxford Union. Josh, Charlie, and Emily were impressed with my fiery conservatism, my passion, and my alarming evidence that Osama was planning nuclear attacks not only on ten cities in America, but also on London. Later that year I got a phone call from them inviting me to speak at the prestigious Oxford Union, in the debating hall that was built in 1824, where Prime Ministers, including the great Winston Churchill have spoken, and American leaders such as Ronald Reagan and Bobby Kennedy have spoken as well! We will tell the story of the Oxford Union American Presidential Debate, and how I was able to warn England of Osama's plans to do a nuclear attack on London, in one of the later chapters in this book.

Not only did we have the Lesser Known Candidates Debate, which was broadcast on C-SPAN all across America and the world, at the Public TV station in Manchester, but the gracious folks there provided a chance for me to be in several debates with other candidates on the public TV station, and to be interviewed on several TV political talk shows, and also, for a very reasonable fee, showed my campaign TV commercial over and over again, 24 times a day (once every hour). And now we come to the crowning achievement, I think, of my entire Presidential campaign, my 30 second TV Campaign Commercial, that we showed on Fox News and CNN in seven states, and on the prime time news slots of CBS national news and Fox 6 local news in Birmingham, my hometown.

Even before the Presidential Primary, I had been looking for ways to get the warning about Osama's American Hiroshima out to America. I had been on dozens of talk radio shows, as I mentioned before I spent thousands of dollars on big ads in the Weekly Standard and the Washington Times, and I wanted to somehow get a TV commercial. The problem was that the TV stations did not want to put a commercial on the air about Osama bin Laden's nuclear attack plans, because "it might scare people." I had talked to my friend John O'Neill, who, along with another of my friends, Jerome Corsi, had co-authored the book Unfit For Command (a very accurate portrayal, by the way, of John Kerry's brief four month navy career in Vietnam). John said the way he and the Swift Boat Vets had gotten their TV ads on the air, where numerous navy veterans who had served with Kerry gave their negative impressions of him, was they made the TV ads, then tried to buy airtime on the major networks, but were denied airtime because of course the liberal media did not want to air anything damaging about their candidate, John Kerry. But then the fact they were denied airtime by the major networks in and of itself became a big news story, and was picked up by all the cable news channels, who showed the Swift Boats ad over and over, for free! (In political terms, I have learned, this is referred to as "earned" media attention, as opposed to "bought" or purchased air time). John O'Neill suggested I try that approach. But I was concerned that perhaps the cable news channels would not pick up the story, and I would have spent a lot of money on an ad about Osama's American Hiroshima that would never see the light of day.

But my Presidential Campaign was the answer to my dilemma. As Steve Kush so brilliantly understood, and executed so well, was that TV stations by law are not allowed to prevent political candidates from purchasing TV airtime and showing their ads, no matter how controversial they are, as long as there is no profanity. So we bought airtime for several weeks on Fox News and CNN (which, as you might imagine, was very expensive) in New Hampshire, the Boston area, which includes Rhode Island and parts of Massachusetts, South Carolina, Texas (including Dallas and Houston), and Alabama. We also showed the ad for weeks right after CBS National News in Birmingham, and during Fox 6 local news in Birmingham. In South Carolina one station tried to block our ad because of its controversial nature, but Steve Kush put the pressure on them, because by law they had to show it even if it was controversial, which makes sense in a free democracy, because if political campaigns are not allowed to talk about controversial topics (and what things in politics are not controversial?) on the air, how can the public ever learn what the issues are?

Again I credit Steve Kush, the consummate political campaign strategist, for making this commercial a reality. He got his friend Rocco, a TV and commercial producer, to meet us in Washington. We filmed the ad on a beautiful sunny day outside the Capitol, a beautiful sunny day reminiscent of Tuesday, September 11, 2001, that dawned so bright and sunny but turned into such a dark day of tragedy. The 30 second TV commercial shows me pointing at the Capitol, saying "Our nation's Capitol is a beautiful sight. But if Osama bin Laden gets his way, this won't be here anymore. I'm Dr. Hugh Cort, Republican Presidential Candidate. I'm a counter-terrorism expert, and we have evidence Osama bin Laden is planning devastating attacks on America, his American Hiroshima plan to blow up ten cities with nuclear devices. To learn more, please check out our website, and vote for me, Dr. Hugh Cort, the only candidate who can prevent this!" and as I point to the Capitol, it blows up in a huge nuclear blast with a mushroom cloud. It is very, very dramatic, and, I am afraid, will come true in the very near future. Some people have accused me of trying to scare America, but I am simply trying to warn America. You can still see my ad today by googling Hugh Cort, and then clicking on Video Results for Hugh Cort – Hugh Cort for President Campaign Ad (from Youtube).

As the New Hampshire Primary drew closer, the media converged on Manchester. All the networks were broadcasting live shows from the hotel I was staying at, and I got to give our info to many of them, including the late Tim Russert. Most notable of all the media people, and the most responsive to our info, was the very impressive and likable Charlie Gibson, the ABC News anchorman. I caught up with him as he was walking briskly through the hotel on the way to the ABC headquarters. I breathlessly and hurriedly was telling him how I had interviewed Hamid Mir, who told us Osama told him he had acquired nuclear suitcase bombs, and I was hurrying because I knew these influential anchormen were under a lot of time pressure. Charles Gibson however, was very gracious, and slowed down to talk with me, and said, "Now relax, and speak slower, so I can understand what you are saying." He spent about ten minutes with me, and I was able to go over our info, plus give him our brochure. I really appreciated his kindness, and the attention he gave our info.

On the eve of the big New Hampshire Presidential Democrat and Republican Debates held back-to-back on ABC, just before the debates started ABC Nightly News came on, and they closed with the story on the Lesser Known Candidates. I was very disappointed they showed Albert Howard's interview instead of mine. But imagine my surprise, and happiness, when the very last thing they showed on ABC Nightly News was the last half of my TV Campaign Commercial, showing me pointing at the Capitol, saying, "and vote for me, Dr. Hugh Cort, the only candidate who can prevent this!" and the Capitol blows up in a huge nuclear blast and mushroom cloud! I had finally got my warning out to the American people! 12 million Americans saw that ad that night. My goal was accomplished!

Then, immediately after the last half of my ad was shown (I guess they thought it was too controversial to show the first half, about Osama's American Hiroshima plan), the big ABC Democrat and Republican Presidential Debates came on, with introductory footage saying, "As our nation faces countless perils, from nuclear suitcase bombs to international crises, which candidate will emerge to lead our country?" They had mentioned, quite prominently, the threat of nuclear suitcase bombs! Steve Kush said, "Doc, you are the one who introduced the topic of nuclear suitcase bombs into the national dialogue. If it wasn't for you, they wouldn't have brought it up!" And also I remembered I had given our counter-terrorism info to fellow Republican candidate Fred Thompson, who, to his great credit, later brought up the threat of nuclear suitcase bombs getting into the hands of terrorists and got it prominently mentioned in the media. And when I was giving my info in September of 2008 out to Senators and their staffers in the Hart Senate Building, I had given my info to then-Senator Obama's staff ,and the next thing I knew a month later Barack Obama brought it up in the Second National Televised Debate with McCain, when he said, "We must stop Osama bin Laden from attacking American cities with suitcase nukes!" And, of course, I am very thankful to the TV thriller show "24" for the episode where a small suitcase nuke explodes in the Los Angeles area, for also helping bring this terrible threat to the attention of the American people. I really have had an effect, on getting the warning out! And it was very gratifying, when I passed George Stephanopoulos on a snowy sidewalk on the way to the hotel where all the TV stations were broadcasting, he said to me, "Dr. Cort, that is a heck of a campaign ad you've got!"

Chapter Six

The Presidential Run, continued: Texas, Rhode Island, Virginia, Wyoming, Georgia, California

The Texas Straw Poll in Ft. Worth was a huge success for our campaign. I was featured to speak along with such notables as fellow Presidential Candidates Duncan Hunter and Ron Paul, Senator John Cornyn, and Michael Steele. Senator John Cornyn, the distinguished Senator from Texas, introduced the debate. Then Congressman Duncan Hunter spoke, then Ron Paul, and then me. I was really happy because they were giving us fourteen minutes to speak, instead of the customary seven minutes typical of most events. I did much better when given more time, because I had so many important points to bring up about Osama's American Hiroshima plan, and other campaign issues such as securing our borders, stopping illegal immigration, a Pro-Life Amendment to the Constitution banning abortion, and a Pro-Marriage Amendment defining marriage as being between a man and a woman only. When I did not feel rushed, I could be relaxed, and really convey and communicate to the audience the evidence we had that Osama bin Laden is planning a devastating nuclear attack on the United States. I was also very strong that we needed to win the War in Iraq, and not pull out like the Democrats and Ron Paul wanted to, and that we desperately needed more troops in Iraq to secure the peace (the wisdom of my strategy was definitely borne out by the success of the Surge, which John McCain, to his eternal credit, was very influential in bringing about).

It would not only be morally wrong to abandon the people of Iraq to be taken over by al Qaeda and Iran, and see all the brave Iraqis who voted, their fingers dipped in ink, have their fingers be cut off by the brutal, evil cowards of al Qaeda and their backers, Ahmadinejad and the Mullahs in Iran, it would also be strategically a huge mistake to abandon Iraq, and let al Qaeda take over. If we did not like Osama and his al Qaeda jihadis training in their terror camps in Afghanistan, how much more would we not like letting them use Iraq as a terrorist playground, with its billions of dollars a year in oil revenues to use to fund their world-wide war of terror? And yes, folks, the Islamo-fascists of Iran and al Qaeda and Syria and Hezbollah and Hamas, and the radical Muslims who support them financially and ideologically, are at war with us, which we will find out for sure, unfortunately too late, when Ayatollah Khamenei achieves his goal of the "destruction of Anglo-Saxon Civilization" and Ahmadinejad as well succeeds in his goal of, as he puts it in speeches around the globe, "soon experiencing a world without the United States and Israel." When Ahmadinejad led a huge crowd of supporters a year ago in a speech at a soccer field in Iran that was broadcast on C-SPAN, where he led hordes of Iranians in a big "Death to America" cheer, chanting over and over, as they angrily shook their fists in the air, "Death to America! Death to America!," he is not bluffing or exaggerating – he means it!

When the numerous Ron Paul supporters in the crowd at the Texas straw poll heard me say we need a troop increase in Iraq, a group of them stood up yelling and hollering, disrupting my speech, because they all wanted to pull out of Iraq and lose the war. As the police confronted them and hauled them out of the hall, I held my fist in the air, shaking my grandfather General Hugh Cort's dogtags, and I shouted, "These are my grandfather's dogtags. He was a General in World War II, and he knew we had to win the war! And we need to win the War in Iraq!" At that, many in the crowd of over two thousand Republican Texas conservatives rose in a huge cheer and gave me a standing ovation! It was one of the greatest moments in my life! Afterward, literally hundreds of delegates came up to me and shook my hand and said, "Dr. Cort, thank you so much for coming to Texas and giving us your counter-terrorism info." The Dallas Morning News had a column the next day, and it was on their internet site also, saying "All the other candidates typically told all the wonderful things they were going to do for America, but Dr. Hugh Cort painted a dark picture of a coming nuclear attack by Osama bin Laden, his American Hiroshima plan to blow up ten cities with suitcase nukes."

I had finally succeeded in getting the words "Osama's American Hiroshima plan" into the mainstream media! And also, it was mentioned in my hometown newspaper, The Birmingham News, in the section where they mention anytime someone from Alabama gets mentioned in the national media. Which helped lead to the one interview The Birmingham News did on my campaign, which we will discuss in the next chapter, on the Presidential Run in my home state of Alabama.

Another great state I had a wonderful Presidential campaign in was Rhode Island. We had been invited to participate in the Rhode Island Straw Poll, the only straw poll held in Rhode Island, in Narragansett. The Republican leaders in the area were young, smart, and well-versed in counter-terrorism issues, and well aware that Osama bin Laden was in no way through with America after 9/11, but that, as former CIA Director George Tenet relates in his book, Ayman al-Zawahiri, the number two man in al Qaeda, said prophetically, "We [al Qaeda] have something much bigger in mind." These intelligent young conservative leaders in Rhode Island were very interested in our counter-terrorism research, and asked us to have dinner with them at a restaurant on the scenic waterfront the night before the Straw Poll. We gave them our info, and they related to us what they had read and heard.

The next night was the Straw Poll. A big crowd gathered in the building right on the beautiful beach. I noticed I was the only Presidential candidate present – all the other candidates had left it up to surrogates to represent them in the speeches. I gave my speech, and I said, "Have you noticed I am the only Presidential candidate who bothered to come to Rhode Island? What do you say you vote for Dr. Hugh Cort, and send the other candidates a message that they'd better not blow off Rhode Island!" The people were all interested in our counter-terrorism info, and Steve and I handed out lots of our brochures. People had bought tickets at a dollar each, to support the Republican Party, and each ticket gave them one vote for the candidate of their choice. The event was a money-raiser for the Republican Party of Rhode Island, so they encouraged folks to buy as many tickets (and as many votes) in support of their candidates as they wanted.

I noticed the surrogate for Mitt Romney, who had been Governor of Massachusetts, right next door to Rhode Island, quietly purchased about $600 worth of tickets. The way the straw poll was set up, they had a preview, "half-time" as it were, count of the votes at about 9:00 PM. Sure enough, Romney was comfortably in the lead at that point, thanks to the hefty contribution of his well-heeled surrogate. However, the surrogate made a fatal mistake. Thinking Romney was now going to win, the surrogate slipped off into the night, off to more exciting things for him than hanging around with a bunch of grassroots Republicans! His mistake, my gain! Steve and I rallied the folks there to vote, and vote often, for the only Presidential candidate who had actually come in person to Rhode Island, Dr. Hugh Cort! And, just to seal the deal, when there were only about three or four minutes left before the final deadline, I wrote a check to the Republican Party to purchase a lot of votes, and when the final tally was counted, with, by the way, the Providence, Rhode Island NBC and ABC TV affiliates filming the count, guess who pulled off the biggest surprise Dark Horse victory in the history of the Rhode Island Straw Poll! None other than yours truly, Dr. Hugh Cort! Later, some scalliwags in some political blogs self-righteously pointed out that multiple votes could be, and were encouraged to be purchased, and that Dr. Cort's generous purchase of votes was what put him over the top. True indeed, but it was legal and strictly within the rules, and when the dust cleared, one salient fact emerged – Dr. Hugh Cort had out-maneuvered, out-lasted, and out-fought every one of the ten major Republican candidates and their surrogates, and had won, fair and square, the Rhode Island Straw Poll, defeating favorite son multi-millionaire Mitt Romney in his own backyard!

On to Virginia! Again, Steve Kush got me a great speaking opportunity, this time at the Virginia Straw Poll, or "the Advance," as they call it in Virginia. I could hardly believe I was sitting there on the front row reserved for the Presidential candidates and their surrogates, waiting my turn to speak. There I was, sitting right beside former Senator and Governor of Virginia, George Allen! A few years earlier I had heard him speak at a very crowded RNC President's Club meeting, back when he was considered the front-runner-to-be in the 2008 Presidential Race, before he suffered defeat in the 2006 Senatorial election. At that time, he seemed to me very regal, Reagan-like, extremely powerful and so high up on the political scene that it was an amazing honor just to be able to squeeze to the front of the crowd, and say a few words to him, and shake his hand. Senator Sam Brownback also spoke that night, and to me, they both seemed so elevated, so high above us mortals, as to be nearly unapproachable. And here now, I was about to speak on the same podium as Senator/ Governor Allen, and when I went across Iowa on The Chairman's Tour with Ray Hoffman and General McInerney, there I was speaking along with Senator Brownback!

As a political junkie, I was in hog heaven! And as a political nobody, a very lesser known candidate, I could not believe I was a speaker, in the company of these famous speakers! It was like some kind of incredible dream! Yet the very thing that drove me to overcome my shyness and embarrassment about my lack of political credentials and go ahead and speak and run for President, my knowledge of the terrible disaster of Osama's nuclear attack that was about to befall America, not only made me speak with conviction, it was my message that was the most important message given that night, or, for that matter, any night of the entire 2008 Presidential Campaign, and the one message America most needed to hear. I prayed to the Lord to take me and speak through me to the crowd and to America.

So there I was, in the speaker's row, sitting next to George Allen, who was just as nice and friendly as he could be. And sitting next to me on the other side was the very nice and sociable Janet Huckabee, wife of Mike Huckabee, to represent him. And next to George was the very gracious Bay Buchanan, sister of Pat Buchanan, who was representing Tom Tancredo, and next to Janet Huckabee was Steve McConnell, the Attorney General of Virginia. Let me say here that, while I was in awe of the distinguished and illustrious political giants I was sitting with, and the other famous political and media giants I have met in the course of my quest to warn America about the coming American Hiroshima, I believe that all people, no matter how famous, are equal in the sight of God. What impressed me was these people were in a position to get my vital info out to America, and speaking at events with them would also help get out my crucial message. I got to speak second, after another former Governor of Virginia, and fellow Presidential Candidate Governor Jim Gilmore spoke, and as I went to the podium I got a warm welcome from John Hager, the valiant Virginia Republican Party Chairman, now retired, and now father-in-law of Jenna Bush, President Bush's daughter. John is a really impressive guy, very dynamic in a statesmanlike, dignified way as he introduced me as a Republican Presidential Candidate, maneuvering around gracefully in his wheelchair (he is semi-paralyzed from polio). As I addressed the huge crowd, giving them the latest info about Osama bin Laden's American Hiroshima plan, I heard the voices of Ron Paul supporters heckling me from the crowd shouting "Osama's dead, Osama's dead!" Wishful thinking, that! I too wish, and wish dearly, that Osama was dead. But I know all too well Osama is alive and well, and he is probably going to succeed in devastating America with his American Hiroshima attack, just like he succeeded in his 9/11 attack. We know from Osama's frequent audiotapes that he is very much alive and well, and the FBI and CIA not only say these audiotapes are authentic, they say there has never been a faked bin Laden tape. Osama bin Laden is alive and well, and he is coming after us, America! Wake up, before it's too late!!!

So I got up, and I spoke, and I warned the people. I had chatted earlier in the crowd with a representative from a town, Red House, Virginia, where Dr. Paul Williams had sent two of our best investigators, Michael Travis and George Samuels, to see what was happening at the Islamic extremist terrorist training camp run by Jamaat-ul-Fuqra in Red House. The representative told me the Muslims there put on the appearance of being peaceful, but he can sense they are "waiting for something" at which time he thinks they will become violent –waiting to play their part in the American Hiroshima? You guessed it! I went off my planned speech for a few minutes, to talk about the Islamic terrorist training camp in Red House, which put the rest of my speech over the time limit, and the organizers had to tell me to finish, that I had gone over my time limit, which was a little embarrassing, but you know, if, God forbid, Osama does do his American Hiroshima attack, and these Muslims in Red House swarm out with their AK-47 assault rifles and open fire and slaughter hundreds of Virginians, they'll wish they had let me go on a little longer in my speech and tell them more about the huge danger that is about to come on them!

Then we went on a campaign trip to Georgia, where I was on TV and in the newspapers all across South Georgia and part of Alabama. Then I went on one of my most memorable trips, to speak to the Republicans of Wyoming, which was going to hold its Republican Primary early, like Nevada in defiance of the RNC, which wanted only the traditionally first Primary states, Iowa and New Hampshire and South Carolina, to go first. The other candidates had visited Wyoming earlier in the year, when the weather was warmer. I had waited until later in the year to decide to go, and when I flew to Cody, Wyoming, I was very concerned that one, I might get snowed in and would not be able to get home to my wife Debbie, who was frail and needed me home as much as possible, and two, I might get stuck in a huge snowdrift and freeze to death driving the long several hours drive from one of the towns I was speaking at back to Cody (and people really do get stuck in blizzards on the road and die in Wyoming sometimes!). Steve Kush could not come on the trip, so I was on my own.

I got a terrific reception in Cody, where I was met at the small airport by the wonderful Carol Armstrong, who had flown around the world with her pilot husband in their small plane years ago on their honeymoon. The next day she took to me to the famous Irma Hotel, built by the legendary William "Buffalo Bill" Cody, who the town of Cody, Wyoming, is named after. The hotel, named after Buffalo Bill's daughter, Irma, is just like you would expect, with a big Western Saloon, with lots of cowboys sitting around the bar in blue jeans and big cowboy hats. I gave my speech to the Republican Women's Club in one of the meeting rooms, and the ladies were sweet and lovely and very politically astute. The mayor of Cody joined us, and a reporter from the biggest newspaper in the region, the Billings, Montana newspaper, came, along with his photographer, and did a great story, fully outlining our vital counter-terrorism info, getting the story out to Wyoming and Montana. If only the Eastern newspapers had reported on Osama's American Hiroshima plan!

The next day, I was treated to a wonderful snowmobile trip to the Wyoming entrance to Yellowstone Park, with a wonderful reporter from the Cody TV station, and two journalists from the Cody newspaper, which also did a great story on me. It was a clear day as we drove the several hours to the Park, but as we steadily ascended upward to the high elevation it began to snow, the first snowfall of the season! It was truly beautiful and magnificent, with the giant pine trees quickly becoming drenched with white in the heavy snowfall. We got onto the snowmobiles and sped across the pristine snow deep into the entrance to the Park, which is several miles. But we had to stop at the rangers' headquarters, because of danger of avalanche. We got off the snowmobiles and had a huge and glorious snowball fight, and the TV reporter's cameraman got a lot of great shots of us all. I made a brief speech about how it was a crying shame some overly-fanatic, whacko "environmentalists" (I believe in preserving the environment, but in a reasonable way, not a whacky, over-done way) were trying to outlaw snow-mobiling in the Park, which is the only way you can really get into the Park in the winter and experience its great, awesome beauty. I changed out of my snow suit back into my regular clothes in a cabin that President George Herbert Walker Bush had stayed in on a trip during his Presidency.

Then we headed back to Cody, after a truly glorious morning and early afternoon! Then I drove off to the town several hours away to give another speech. The roads in Wyoming are long and lonely, and I was very glad a blizzard did not happen that day (a big one came the very next day!). The scenery was breathtaking, with the tall mountain ranges ringing the desolate plains, in places looking a little like the surface of the moon, and hardly a car on the road, the little towns few and far between. I gave my speech to an enthusiastic crowd, and got a few votes in the little straw poll they held, then made my way back to Cody. I was so thankful it was not snowing, and I would be able to get back to Cody safe and sound, and fly back to my Debbie the next morning. I called Debbie on the cell phone, and we had a wonderful, long talk, as I drove the miles back to Cody. Thank God for cell phones! Aren't they wonderful? There I was, in the wilds of Wyoming, talking to my sweet Debbie all the way back in Alabama! I'll remember the wonderful long sweet phone call with Debbie the rest of my life.

I got up at four in the morning in order to catch the 6 AM flight out of Cody, and I was very glad I had got up early, because it had just started snowing, and an hour later I could not have made it to the airport. Even so, I was worried I would not be able to make it, because the snow was already three inches deep and falling fast as I headed to the airport. But to my surprise, in the early pre-dawn darkness, here came the City of Cody snowplows, whirling and wheeling through the streets, making a way clear to the main road and the airport! I was so grateful to God for sending those valiant snowplows to the rescue! I drove carefully on the snowy streets and gratefully made it to the airport. I was still a little afraid the plane would not be able to take off in the snowstorm, but we bulled down the runway in the small propeller plane, and thanks to God, lifted off! I was never so happy to be airborne! Once again, our dear God had blessed me and Debbie, and I was able to get home to her and not be stuck for days in Wyoming!

Another great campaign trip was to beautiful Northern California, to give a speech at the Lake County Republican Party Shin-dig. We flew into Sacramento and were met by the friendly Republican County Chairman Steve Davis, who drove us to his beautiful home in Lake County, overlooking the biggest lake in California and an extinct volcano! There his lovely wife Elizabeth fixed us a bountiful supper. That night they took us outside and showed us the Milky Way, extending all across the Northern California sky. The air in Lake County has been judged the third clearest air in the country, which is why the Milky Way was so incredibly visible. Quite a change from L.A.! The next morning we had a great adventure, when Steve took us out to his friend's 350 acre buffalo ranch! We tracked the herd of about fifty buffalo until we could get close enough for a shot (a camera shot – Steve's friend asked if I wanted to shoot with a camera or a rifle, and I chose the camera, since I was not going to be there at that ranch in the evening for dinner, and I don't like to kill an animal unless I am going to eat it). It is amazing how difficult it is to sneak up close to a buffalo herd – they are very astute and skitterish, and every time you get close, they take off over the next hill – makes you appreciate how much the Indians went through when they would hunt buffalo! Then later we had some target practice – I was proud to hit the distant target, a rock, two out of three times. I'm a pretty good shot, if I do say so myself!

Then Steve Davis, the consummate host, took us to another friend who took us on a boat trip across the big lake. It was a beautiful, sunny day, and when we got across the lake we had a delicious lunch at the new winery there. Lake County is just north of Napa County, and there are some beautiful vineyards there. Finally it was time for the big shin-dig, a Western style barbecue at a beautiful farm with acres of luscious green grass, a pond and lovely willow trees. The gorgeous California sunshine saturated the atmosphere in an almost surreal way – the perfectly clear air of Lake County gave the sunshine an incredible, dreamlike golden quality I have never seen before – I must say it is true what they say about "California sunshine!" Lots of people arrived in Western attire for the barbecue and auction, and then I addressed the crowd, giving them our alarming info about Osama's coming nuclear attack on America. I hated to dampen such a beautiful evening, but it is my duty to warn America, and I dutifully told them, all of them red-blooded American gun-owners, that we are for sure going to need our guns if, after Osama's men blow up downtown Los Angeles with a nuclear weapon, Osama's terrorist "sleepers" burst out in the suburbs with AK 47's blazing away, Mumbai-style. I told them what Adam Gadahn, the son of a California goat-herder who went to Pakistan and joined al Qaeda and became their media guru (also known as "the American al Qaeda, or Azzam the American), said about the coming conflict –"The streets of Los Angeles will run red with blood!"

Chapter Seven

The Presidential Run, continued: Sweet Home Alabama!

I definitely wanted to get on the ballot in my home state of Sweet Home Alabama. It was not an easy process, but, with God all things are possible, and with His help we got on the Republican Presidential Primary ballot. I had to pay $5,000 to the Republican Party of Alabama, and I had to get 500 signatures on a petition advocating my candidacy, like all the other candidates. It was a lot more work to get all the signatures than I had imagined – it is very tiring going up to folks and getting them to sign, especially if you are tired from all the multi-state campaigning and frequent trips around the nation I was going on. Fortunately I had a lot of help – my South Carolina Co-Campaign Chairmen, Dean Allen and George Mabry, came from South Carolina to Alabama to help us. My Alabama Campaign Chairman, attorney Ted Pearson, helped us. A wonderful elderly black woman, Willie Mae Brown, who has since gone home to be with the Lord, who liked our "Get America Back to God" campaign theme, got a lot of signatures. But nobody got near as many as the amazing Minzor Chadwick, who put us over the top, single-handedly getting over 500 signatures by himself! Minzor is legally blind from optic atrophy, but that has not slowed him down at all from protesting almost every day for seventeen years at the abortion mills in Birmingham (there used to be seven, and now, Praise God, there are only two, even if they are still two too many). Minzor has saved the lives of many children from abortion by giving their mothers who were heading into the abortion clinic information about how Sav-A-Life will support them financially, and help them have their baby, and then help them keep the baby, or find a good home for the baby, whichever they wish, and the mothers changed their minds and decided not to abort their children! Minzor had a real knack for getting people to sign our petition, plus a dedicated, hard-working spirit to accomplish the goal and get me on the ballot.

The local CBS TV affiliate reporter, Mike McClanahan, was really great, doing three news clips on our campaign, including showing video from one of our South Carolina campaign speeches, and showing me chatting with Ron Paul back-stage just before we gave our speeches. The Birmingham News had one of their political reporters do an article on my campaign, but he was a real reprobate, and went out of his way to distort my words, and even tell a bald-faced lie, to try to portray me as a nut-case who was trying to scare the country. When he interviewed me, he tried to bully me, forcefully and angrily criticizing my Pro-Life stance, saying, "How can you think America cares about stopping abortion? Polls show most Americans favor abortion." This is an outright lie: recent polls show over 50% of Americans are against abortion, and if the Satan-controlled media ever had the decency to show what really happens in an abortion, show an ultra-sound on TV, and Americans saw the unborn baby scream in agony as its arms and legs are torn off by the abortionist's forceps, or worse yet, if they would show a video of a partial-birth abortion, which despite being outlawed by Congress still happens 5,000 times a year thanks to some court orders of liberal judges, and Americans saw the partially born baby, its body out of the womb except for its head, jerk its arms and legs out in a spasm of agony as the abortionist stabs a hole in the back of its neck, so he can insert the vacuum hose into the skull and suction out the brains in order to get the baby's head to collapse so he can finally pull it out of the birth canal, Americans would vote overwhelmingly to stop the travesty, the holocaust of abortion!

Then this reprobate reporter very angrily and forcefully bullied me some more, saying, about my Pro-Marriage stance, "Don't you know the great majority of Americans are in favor of gay marriage?" I told him that is not true at all, and even if it were, it would not make gay marriage pleasing to God, if we believe what God says in the Bible about it. This seemed to make him even madder. I thought news reporters, especially political reporters, were supposed to keep their personal prejudices to themselves, and just report the facts objectively and truthfully, but not this guy! I guess all the frustration for years of having to report the news, instead of being one of the people who makes the news, was boiling over in this fire-breathing liberal! Then he rudely tried to dismiss our counter-terrorism info, and did not even mention in the article my interview of Hamid Mir, the Pakistani journalist who found that Osama bin Laden had acquired suitcase nuclear bombs, or my conversation with Yossef Bodansky, former Director of the Congressional Task on Terrorism for 16 years, who told me the same thing, or any of our other evidence. Instead, this reprobate, violating all the rules of objective journalism, twisted and distorted and changed my words to try to make my assertions look foolish – for example, when I told him Dr. Paul Williams' interviews of Mexican drug smugglers had shown there was a very strong possibility that suitcase nukes were smuggled through the some of the numerous tunnels the drug smugglers have dug under the Mexican border (our Border Patrol has found more than 34 of these tunnels, and Anderson Cooper on CNN 360 has shown us one tunnel big enough to drive a truck through), this reprobate Birmingham News rogue reporter wrote in his article that I said "The bombs were smuggled through long tunnels from Mexico into American cities," implying that I thought there were tunnels hundreds of miles long extending from Mexico all the way to the target cities, which would be absurd. No, the tunnels are short, going from the Mexican side of the border to the American side, where once the smugglers get through, and have eluded the Border Patrol's scrutiny, they load up their drugs and illegal humans in trucks and proceed on their way.

Another way this rogue reporter tried to falsely discredit me and try to make me look nutty and irrational, was to say I was totally convinced I would win the Presidency, which of course was not true. At the start of the interview he very forcefully tried to bully me, getting in my face and sneering aggressively, "You don't have a chance to win." I said, because I don't let anyone push me around, "I think I have a chance to win" (even if a very, very small chance – and you know, it's really too bad America didn't listen, and I didn't win, because truly I was the only candidate who was aware of the huge threat coming our way from al Qaeda and Iran, and the only candidate willing to bring it up and try to stop it). Then he said again, even louder and meaner, "No, you don't have a chance." Then I said, "I think I have a chance, even if a small chance." I went on to say, "I realize I am most likely not going to win, and that is okay with me, because the real reason I am running is to get the warning about Osama's American Hiroshima attack out to the people of America, not to get votes." So guess how this lying reprobate wrote the article? He told an out-and-out, bald-faced lie, writing, "Dr. Cort is totally convinced he is going to win the election for President of the United States," which of course made me sound like a very irrational person.

I very seriously thought about suing him for lying about me and purposefully distorting my words in order to discredit me, but I was very busy traveling around the country campaigning, and I just did not have the energy or the time to fool with such a reprobate. However, it is still a possibility to sue this guy for malpractice of journalism and lying and slander, if the Lord should lead me to sue him. But I remember the Lord's words in the Bible, "Vengeance is mine, saith the Lord. I will repay, saith the Lord." I will let God deal with this reprobate, because God can deal with him a lot better than me. I hope and pray we are wrong about Osama's nuclear attack – I desperately hope he does not have suitcase nukes in our country, or if he does, I hope they turn out to be duds. But if God forbid, Osama bin Laden does accomplish his goal of destroying ten American cities with nuclear bombs, like he accomplished his goal of attacking the World Trade Center Towers, I hope that reporter, and the rest of the news media, regrets that they were warned, but did not do their job and warn America!

I did get some better press coverage from the other newspapers in the State of Alabama-The Huntsville Times, The Montgomery Advertiser, The Mobile Press Register, and the

Gulf Coast Newspaper Chain, where reporter Bob Morgan did the best in-depth, thorough, objective report of my campaign and our counter-terrorism information.

I got on TV news in Huntsville, Birmingham, Montgomery, and Mobile. I got to speak at several places in Alabama, although my campaigning was heaviest in the early primary states. I enjoyed speaking to the Mobile County Republicans, and the Kiwanis Club in Florence, among other places.

My brother, Charles Cort, campaigned heavily for me in Mobile and Baldwin County, and I appreciated his kind support very much! Charles also wrote letters to the editor to forty newspapers in Texas, about my strong stand on border security and illegal immigration, which helped me get a lot of votes in Texas.

Chapter Eight

The Oxford Union – Dr. Cort Warns England!

Imagine my surprise when, shortly after John McCain was nominated to be the Republican candidate for President, and Barack Obama was nominated as the Democrat candidate, I got a phone call at my office from Charlie Holt, the President-elect of the Oxford Union, the prestigious English debating society at Oxford University! Charlie said the officers of the Oxford Union had seen me speak on the issues in the Lesser Known Presidential Candidates Debate on C-SPAN that was held in New Hampshire, and they wanted me to speak at their American Presidential Debate in October, arguing in favor of John McCain, the Republican Candidate. I was in awe – the Oxford Union! The world famous debating society where Members of Parliament, Prime Ministers of England, Winston Churchill, Ronald Reagan, Bobby Kennedy, and Albert Einstein have debated and spoken! Of course I told Charlie, "Yes, I will come speak at the Oxford Union!"

I was especially happy about this because I felt the Lord was giving me a chance to warn England that it was also being targeted for nuclear attack by Osama bin Laden. Hamid Mir had told us that his contacts had told him that Osama, in addition to targeting ten American cities, was also targeting London, Paris, Rome, (and possibly Copenhagen as well), for nuclear attack. Remember, Hassan Abassi, one of Iran's Supreme Leader Khamenei's top advisors, had said that "We Iranians have devised a strategy for the destruction of Anglo-Saxon Civilization," and another Iranian official said "We already have 37 sites picked out in America and elsewhere in the West [meaning our allies in England and Europe] and we know how we are going to attack them." If you look at our colleague Ryan Mauro's interview of Hamid Mir, on the topic of Osama bin Laden's Nuclear Arsenal that is in the back of this

67

book in the Appendix, you will see where Hamid Mir reports that Osama is going to have a nuclear suitcase bomb sent to his people in London, to detonate at the same time as he does the American Hiroshima attack in America. Another sign is that Adnan Shukrijumah, the nuclear technician who is the ringleader of Osama's American Hiroshima plan, has been reported by intelligence authorities to have made a trip to London. Add to this the report in November 2008 from England's National Security Advisor Lord West that al Qaeda is planning a "spectacular attack" in the near future, and that "the threat is huge," and you can clearly see that England, our ally in the War on Terror in Iraq and Afghanistan, is in danger of nuclear attack just as we are here in America!

When I arrived in London, I decided to take one day in London to bring my warning that London was targeted by Osama for nuclear attack to as many authorities as I could. I only had one day in London, because I had to get up to Oxford, about an hour and a half train ride away, to prepare for the Oxford Debate. I wondered what I could accomplish in just one day, but I prayed for the Lord to use me, and boy, did He accomplish a lot! I started out the day eating breakfast at the Kensington Hilton, and I got a copy of the London Times to read during breakfast. Well, there on the front page was a story by the counter-terrorism reporters for the Times, Dominic Kennedy and Richard Kerbaj, on how British Intelligence MI6 had discovered that al Qaeda was using encrypted messages on child pornography sites to convey information to various al Qaeda cells around the world (a month earlier ABC News reported in their "October Surprise?" TV story, that our Intelligence Agencies had intercepted a message sent by al Qaeda High Command to all the local al Qaeda cells around the world by <u>encrypted messages</u> and couriers, saying "Be on notice. We may call upon you soon.").

I took a London cab to the Times of London newspaper office, an imposing walled structure much like a fortress. I went to the security guard at the gate, and explained who I was, and that I would like a chance to give some important counter-terrorism information to Dominic Kennedy and Richard Kerbaj. The guard laughed at me, and said, "Sir, no one ever gets in to see a reporter without an appointment!" I persevered, and said, "Just let me talk to Dominic or Richard on the phone for a minute, and I know they will want to see me." The security guard finally agreed to get them on the phone. I told them I was Dr. Hugh Cort, President of the American Foundation for Counter-Terrorism Policy and Research, and I work with General Tom McInerney (thank you, General McInerney, for agreeing to be an honorary board member – your well-deserved name and reputation as a counter-terrorism expert has opened many a door for me to get our vital information heard!) I told them I had interviewed in person Hamid Mir, the Pakistani journalist who has interviewed Osama bin Laden three times. And I told them I had information that Osama bin Laden was planning a nuclear attack on London. The journalists told the guard, "Let him in!" The guard had a shocked expression on his face as he let me in the well-fortified doorway, murmuring, "I can't believe it! Twenty years, and I've never seen a person get inside without an appointment!"

I spent two hours giving Dominic and Richard our info, and I also gave them a copy of Paul Williams' great book <u>The Day of Islam: The Annihilation of America and the Western World</u>, that gives so much highly detailed, factual evidence that Iran and Osama are planning devastating nuclear, chemical, and biological attacks (please read it – you can order a copy from Barnes and Noble or Amazon.com or Books-A-Million, or any bookseller). They were very interested, and gave me their email addresses, and I send them any new information that comes in.

Then I took a cab to the office of the Mayor of London, on the banks of the Thames River, or The River Thames, as they call it. The Mayor's office is a modern art type building that truly looks, and I am not exaggerating, for all the world like a giant beehive! You have to see it to believe it! I went to the top floor, and gave our info to the Mayor's staff. They can't say they haven't been warned that London is a target of a nuclear terrorist attack!

Then I strolled through the scenic streets by the banks of the River Thames to my next stop on the counter-terrorism trail, the imposing offices of British Intelligence, MI6 (the British counterpart of our CIA). I told the security guard my business, and he told me to wait a minute, and he would get some staff to come talk with me. The next thing I knew, there were two heavily armed military looking fellows with short, sawed off sub-machine guns, who were polite, but very very serious as they questioned me. They looked a little nervous when I opened my briefcase, but relaxed when they saw that all that was in there were papers. I gave them our brochure (you can see the same info on our website, www.afcpr.org) with our information about a possible nuclear terrorist attack on London and America, and as I explained our sources, they realized this was something important. They were very interested, and took the information, and said they were going to pass it along to some higher-ups inside. I mentioned that I wanted to also get the info to MI5 (the British counterpart to our FBI) and to Scotland Yard, the Police Headquarters of London. They said the higher-ups inside, who they were going to bring our info, would certainly pass it along to MI5 and to Scotland Yard. I thanked them, and walked away, a little bit glad to get away from those threatening looking sub-machine guns!

My next stops were to two other British newspapers, The Telegraph and The Daily Mail. At each newspaper I made contact by phone with the chief counter-terrorism reporters, and explained our info, and the reporters sent couriers to the lobby to get our brochure and other info. Then I went to Parliament. I had hoped to get in to give some info to some Members of Parliament, but it was getting late in the day and they said it was too late to go inside. However I did get to give our brochure and other info to the security folks who said they would pass it on. I was a little disappointed I had not made contact with any Members of Parliament, but fortunately I was able to meet several students later that week at the Oxford Union who either worked part time doing research for Members of Parliament, or had contacts with them. So I felt I had put in a pretty good day of it and with God's help, accomplished a lot – got our info and Paul Williams' book <u>The Day of Islam</u> (you gotta read this book!) to the main counter-terrorism reporters at one of the biggest newspapers in England, the Times of London; got our info to the Mayor of London's staff, got it to British Intelligence MI6, and through them to MI5 and Scotland Yard (now, as in the past, Scotland Yard desperately needs the help of Sherlock Holmes, and I was able to connect them with the modern day version of Sherlock Holmes, my colleague, Dr. Paul Williams!); got our info to the reporters who cover terrorism issues at two other major British newspapers, and left our info with Security to pass on to Parliament! Not bad for a day's work, eh?!

The next day I got on the bus headed for historic Oxford University! I disembarked at famous Gloucester Green, a charming little cobblestone brick square lined with trees, on a nice fall day with a little bit of sunshine (a rare thing in England—on my previous trip to England in August it had rained a steady drizzle for 13 out of 16 days!). I made my way to ancient Corn Market Street, the main thoroughfare in Oxford, and soon was at my hotel, the delightful and quaint Randolph Hotel, just across the street from the famous New Ashmolean history museum. After leaving my suitcase in my room, I walked through the ancient streets to the historic Oxford Union, where I met with the President of the Oxford Union, the intelligent and affable Josh Roche, Charlie Holt, the President-elect, who would become President in 2009, and Luke Tryl, the 2007 President. They were very cordial and helpful during my entire week's stay. Luke took me to sit in on one of his political science classes, and also introduced me to Bilawal Zardari, son of Pakistani President Zardari, who attends college at Oxford. Bilawal took me out to lunch, where we had a great, long discussion of Pakistani politics (he knows my friend Pakistani journalist Hamid Mir very well) and Bilawal caught me up on all the political turmoil that has been going on in Pakistan since the tragic assassination of his lovely mother Benazir Bhutto, and I was able to acquaint him with Osama bin Laden's plans for a nuclear attack on America and England.

A few days before the Debate I was interviewed by Alistair Walker, reporter for the big Oxford student newspaper. He did a great interview, which was on the front page, with a big photo of myself, with the whimsical title "Osama's Suitcase Full O' Nukes" which got a lot of attention! Everyone at Oxford University now knows that Osama bin Laden is planning a nuclear attack on London. The day before the big debate I went for a long walk by the peaceful Thames River, past soccer fields and fishermen and folks in little houseboats by the water's side. That evening I went to the local BBC Radio and TV station, where I had been invited to do a radio interview with one of the well-known talk radio show hosts. We had a lively on-air discussion of Osama's plans for a nuclear attack, and I gave him our info and, of course, Dr. Williams' book, The Day of Islam, which he said he would pass along to the BBC Television folks. Also I got to give out over the British radio airwaves our website, www.afcpr.org, so the English people can see for themselves the evidence that Osama and Iran are planning for the nuclear devastation of London (please see our website so you, too, can be fully informed of the danger that is soon to come upon America and England, and France and Italy and Germany, and perhaps Copenhagen and elsewhere – Osama is angry at these countries for assisting us in Iraq and Afghanistan. As Osama said in an audiotape recently, he is threatening retaliation on European countries, including England, for assisting America in Afghanistan.

Finally came the day of the big Oxford Union Debate! That afternoon, I went to the historic Oxford Union debating hall, built in 1824, to do a practice run-through of my speech. I felt a powerful sense of awe as I walked onto the hardwood floor, and looked up at the galleries which hold about six hundred people, and gazed at the portraits that hung on the walls of former Prime Ministers and Members of Parliament who have spoken on the same floor upon which I was standing! There was Gladstone, the famous Prime Minister, and over there, Winston Churchill, and all around one hundred and eighty-nine years of English history brought to mind by the famous leaders of Britain! As I spoke the first lines of my speech, hearing my words resonate in the perfect acoustics of the hall, I felt a thrill that I was speaking on the very floor where Albert Einstein explained to the students his Theory of Relativity, and Ronald Reagan won his historic debate with Bobby Kennedy, and Winston Churchill's son in 1934 urged the crowd to stop Hitler's war machine before it got too big, and where Winston Churchill himself urged England to fight on and never give up!

That evening, before the Debate, the leadership of the Oxford Union had a big dinner party for me and my debate opponent, well-known liberal David Mixner, who would be arguing in favor of Barack Obama, and the students who were going to be on our debate teams. David Mixner was very friendly and cordial. Liberals are often very friendly, nice people—they're just so <u>wrong</u> about the issues! The photographer came and took pictures of all of us—the picture will hang on the wall along with the pictures of Albert Einstein and Ronald Reagan and Churchill and all the other famous people who have spoken at the Union!

Finally the debate started. The hall, seating over six hundred, was soon jammed with students (the British people are keenly interested in American politics). First, a student took the floor to debate in favor of the American Democrat candidate for President, Barack Obama. These British students are really amazing in their oratorical skills. I was very impressed by their intuitive grasp of the English language; after all, this is the land of Chaucer, William Shakespeare, Longfellow, and the other bards! Then he sat down, and another student, this time on my side of the bench, got up and argued eloquently in favor of John McCain. I was to have been joined by my friend Jerry Corsi, who wrote the best-selling book <u>The Obama Nation,</u> to debate on my side for John McCain, but he was unable to come due to illness and exhaustion he sustained after being detained in jail in Kenya when researching the family of Barack Obama.

Then the second student spoke on behalf of Obama, and again, he was very eloquent. Then the second student spoke from my side of the bench. Timothy Stafford, who is a truly great orator, was magnificent in his speech that McCain was the one with the experience needed in a dangerous world full of Islamic terrorists and rogue states who support terrorism like Iran and North Korea. Then Josh, the President of the Union, called upon any students in the audience who wished to speak, to make comments, and several students brought up some really good points.

Finally, it time for us "big guns", as it were, the Americans! First David Mixner spoke, a very passionate and heartfelt speech in favor of Obama. He got a huge applause from the highly partisan crowd (most English students, indeed most Europeans, are very liberal, and are not able to see the cable news shows and conservative talk radio we Americans are blessed to get, and they have a very one-sided view of the issues). Then it was my turn.

I thanked the large crowd for their attendance in this great hall of English history, the famous Oxford Union. I thanked the illustrious leadership of the Oxford Union that had invited me to come across the Atlantic to participate in the Debate. Then I started my speech, contrasting McCain's years of experience with Barack Obama's lack of experience. I said, "Senator McCain has twenty-two years of experience in the Senate. Barack Obama, who has been campaigning for the past two years, essentially has only two years of actual work in the Senate, during which time he has accomplished virtually nothing of importance. How many of you students, if your parents or grandparents should need open heart bypass surgery, would chose a surgeon with only two years of experience?

Wouldn't you rather choose a surgeon with twenty-two years of experience?"

Then I told them how Iran has not only threatened to "wipe Israel off the face of the Earth" in a second, and this time final Holocaust, but has also said, "We Iranians have devised a strategy for the destruction of Anglo-Saxon Civilization, and we know how we are going to attack them!" And Ahmadinejad constantly gives speeches where he says, "We will soon experience a world without the United States!" and leads crowds of hundreds of thousands of Iranians in "Death to America" cheers! And FBI Director Robert Mueller has testified to Congress that Iran's terror network, Hezbollah, has now come through the porous Mexican border, and is now in our country! And Iran has been planning, along with their ally Osama bin Laden, not only an American Hiroshima that will devastate ten cities in America with nuclear bombs, but a nuclear attack on London, Paris, and Rome as well!

Then I said, "Winston Churchill's son stood in this very hall and said "We must stop Hitler before his war machine gets too big, before it is too late!" but England and France and America didn't listen, and Hitler grew his "Wehrmacht", his war machine, to a huge, almost unstoppable size, and when he over-ran the continent of Europe, and nearly conquered England, and finally America joined in, it took 62 million people to die in World War II to finally stop Hitler. If we don't stop Iran from getting nuclear weapons, they will start nuclear World War III, and it will take 200 million people to die to stop them! I paused, and in a strong voice proclaimed, "The year is 1939, Ahmadinejad is Hitler, and if Winston Churchill were here tonight he would beg you to stop Iran from getting nuclear weapons before it's too late!" The students, liberal though they were, gave me a tremendous, thundering round of applause, realizing the terrible threat that a nuclear Iran poses to the world.

Then I explained to them all of our counter-terrorism info, about how Osama and Iran are targeting America and London for nuclear attack in the near future. I told them what to do if they or their friends and families should be in the area of London when the nuclear bomb explodes, and how to avoid radiation poisoning, and take potassium iodide pills to avoid thyroid cancer which a radioactive iodine from a nuclear blast can cause even three hundred miles downwind. I told them that just as God had sent my grandfather, General Hugh Cort, and the American army, to England during her darkest hour, to save her from destruction by the Nazis, I felt God has sent me here tonight, to warn you, and help you survive, the coming nuclear attack of Osama bin Laden. Then I closed with "God bless you, God bless America, and God bless the U.K.!"

I got a lot of applause. Then they had the vote, and McCain only got 50 votes, and Barack Obama got 550! I shook hands with the crowd as they filed out, and gave them each a brochure on our counter-terrorism info. Then I went to the after-party the leadership of the Oxford Union held in the upstairs of the historic building that is adjacent to the speaking hall. The leadership of the Oxford Union, unlike the majority of Oxford University students who attended the debate, is very conservative, many of their parents are conservative Members of Parliament (MP's), and they loved my speech, and loved the way I "took it to the liberals!" A very beautiful and gracious young lady, Miss Emily Gardner, said it all, and absolutely made my night when she enthusiastically exclaimed, "You're a legend, Dr. Cort!"

Chapter Nine

The Hunt for Shukrijumah
(The Next Mohammed Atta)

Who is Adnan Shukrijumah? FBI Director Robert Mueller calls him "the next Mohammed Atta," the leader of the next 9/11, Osama's nuclear attack, the American Hiroshima. Just as Osama bin Laden chose Mohammed Atta to lead the 9/11 hijackers, he has chosen Adnan Shukrijumah, a trained nuclear technician, to lead his coming nuclear attack, which, according to the Arabic newspaper Al-Quds Al-Arabi, will be "far bigger than 9/11" and will "change the economic and political structure of the world" and "will happen in the near future." Remember, Al-Quds Al-Arabi is the same newspaper that published a statement by Osama three weeks before 9/11 saying he "was going to attack America in an unprecedented way" and then three weeks later he did 9/11. Now here is the same newspaper, predicting a much bigger attack, in the near future!

Adnan el-Shukrijuma is the son of radical, extremist Muslim Imam Gulshair el-Shukrijumah, who first preached at the infamous Farouq Mosque in Brooklyn, where a lot of the planning for the first World Trade Center bombing in 1993, and also for 9/11 went on, a mosque, as Paul Williams writes, "that raised millions for the jihad and that served as a recruiting station for al Qaeda"[24] (a mosque that still operates today, and which is very secretive, threatening bodily harm or worse to Paul Williams when he tried to enter the mosque). Gulshair later moved to Miramar, Florida, where he became the Imam of another radical Islamic mosque. It was there that Adnan "became friends with José Padilla, who planned to detonate a radiological bomb in midtown Manhattan, Mandhai Jokhan, who was convicted of attempting to blow up nuclear power plants in southern Florida, and a group of other home-grown terrorists." Paul Williams goes on to report, 'Adnan attended flight schools in Florida and Norman, Oklahoma, along with Mohammed Atta and the other 9/11 operatives."[25] He was originally going to be one of the 9/11 pilots, but Osama held him out of the 9/11 attack in order to lead the American Hiroshima, which Osama had been planning long before 9/11 (he first started seeking nuclear materials and nuclear weapons in 1992). Yes, 9/11 was just a shot across the bow, a wake-up call to America to let it know the war was on – the coming American Hiroshima is the finishing blow, Osama's grand finale, still to come, and soon!

Dr. Paul Williams continues to write, "El-Shukrijumah became singled out by bin Laden and al-Zawahiri to serve as the field commander for the next great attack on American soil – the so-called American Hiroshima – that would leave millions dead and the richest and most powerful nation on earth in ashes. In preparation for this mission, Adnan, along with fellow al Qaeda sleeper agents Anas al-Liby, Jaber A. Elbaneh (whose uncle was the Imam of the infamous mosque in Buffalo associated with "The Lackawanna Seven" terrorist money-raisers), and Amer el-Maati, was sent to McMaster University in Hamilton, Ontario, a facility that boasted a five-megawatt nuclear research reactor, the largest reactor of any educational facility in Canada. At McMaster, where they may have enrolled under aliases, el-Shukrijumah and his associates wasted little time gaining access to the nuclear reactor and stealing more than 180 pounds of nuclear waste for the creation of radiological bombs."[26]

For writing this in his book, and talking about it on some talk radio shows, Dr. Williams was warned by McMaster University to retract his claims, or else face a lawsuit. Dr. Williams refused to be intimidated, and pressed ahead, even welcoming a lawsuit because that would give him the legal right to discovery, which means he and his lawyers can get into McMasters' records, which they have been refusing to allow anyone to look at, to ascertain if Shukrijumah may have used some of his many aliases (Abu Arifi, Jafar al-Tayyar, which means Jafer the Pilot, and Mohammed Sher Mohammed Khan) to enroll as a student at McMaster. Dr. Williams has spent $50,000 of his own money in legal fees to pursue this case and get to the truth, and force McMaster to open their files, and he goes to Canada in October, 2009 to testify in the preliminary phase to the trial. Dr. Williams hopes this trial will break the case open in the Canadian media, which will force the sedentary American media to report on it, which hopefully may bring the vital topic of Osama bin Laden's American Hiroshima attack to the attention of the American people. Do you see a pattern here? Dr. Williams and I are breaking our backs, spending all our money, doing everything we possibly can to warn the American people about the nuclear devastation that is soon to come upon them, but we can't get the media to even take a look at it! If you would like to donate to the Paul Williams Defense Fund, just go to our websites, www.afcpr.org, or www. stopdoomsday.com and click on the Paul Williams Defense Fund button, or go to www. paulwilliamsdefensefund.com.

When Khalid Sheikh Mohammed, Osama's master-planner for 9/11, was captured, and he told the CIA and the Pakistani Intelligence, and this was on his computer as well, that Osama bin Laden was planning a "nuclear hell storm" in America, he said the chain of command was bin Laden, al-Zawahiri, and a scientist, "Dr. X" [the infamous Dr. Abdul Qadeer Khan, the father of Pakistan's "Islamic bomb" who has given nuclear bomb technology to every rogue nation in the world]. He went on to say that the field commander was a naturalized American citizen whom he called "Jafer al-Tayyar" (Jafer the Pilot), also known as (aka) Adnan Shukrijumah.[27]   If you go to the FBI website at www.fbi.gov, you can see Adnan Shukrijumah's wanted poster, with his mug-shot and a 5 million dollar reward on his head. The FBI reports Shukrijumah was at a terrorist conference in the Waziristan Province of Pakistan where he and other al Qaeda leaders were planning the American Hiroshima. The FBI has described the conference as a "pivotal planning session" just like a similar conference in Kuala Lumpur was the pivotal planning session for 9/11.

Shukrijumah has been spotted in Mexico, where he is believed to have been enlisting the help of a Latino street gang, Mara Salvatrucha (MS-13), which smuggles drugs and humans through the Mexican border into the U.S., to help him smuggle Osama's suitcase nuclear bombs into America. As Dr. Williams writes, "Concern about el-Shukrijumah's sojourn in Mexico was heightened with the arrest in Pakistan of Sharif al-Masri, a key al Qaeda operative. Al-Masri, an Egyptian national with close ties to Ayman al-Zawahiri, informed interrogators that al Qaeda has made arrangements to smuggle small tactical nuclear weapons [suitcase nukes] into Mexico. From Mexico, the weapons were to be transported across the border with the help of a Latino street gang" (Mara Salvatrucha, or MS-13, as it is more commonly known).[28] Dr. Williams has interviewed a Mara Salvatrucha gang member who believes el-Shukrijumah has already brought nuclear bombs into the U.S., and that "plans for the next 9/11 are well under way, and it is too late for U.S. officials to prevent the coming nuclear nightmare." The gang member goes on to say he has transported dozens of illegals from Middle Eastern countries (Special Interest Aliens, or SIA's, a type of OTM's, or Other-Than-Mexicans) who he believes are terrorists coming in to participate in the big attack.[29]

So why am I mentioning all this about Osama's ringleader for the American Hiroshima, Adnan Shukrijumah? Because he represents one of the best chances we have to "break the case" and stop Osama's American Hiroshima! If we can catch the elusive Shukrijumah, who is a master of disguise, we can trace the other operatives, and possibly stop the next 9/11! We think Shukrijumah is headquartered in the Toronto area, in a suburb called Mississauga, and he periodically sneaks in to America to meet with his sleeper agents in the ten cities who have the suitcase nukes hidden in their basements, to help them maintain the bombs, which require some maintenance about every six months. If we can catch him, perhaps through his computer or cell phone we can catch the others, and locate the bombs before it's too late.

So how do we catch Shukrijumah? Dr. Williams and Laurice Tatum, a private investigator who has worked with the FBI and who is the secretary of our counter-terrorism foundation (AFCPR.org), and I have made several trips to Ontario, Canada to hunt for Shukrijumah. Although we have come close a time or two, we have not yet been able to catch him. Michael Travis, who is also a board member of AFCPR.org, and Sean Michaels, an anchor for the huge Canadian TV network Global TV, have made several trips to McMaster and elsewhere in Ontario. The FBI has been trying to catch Shukrijumah for over five years, but despite a 5 million dollar reward on his head, they have not been able to find him. There are only 12,000 FBI agents in the country – no wonder they can't find him. But if they would put his face on "America's Most Wanted" TV show, 300 million Americans and 36 million Canadians could find the guy in two weeks! I have gone to California to meet in person with one of "America's Most Wanted" TV show producers, and I have contacted the show numerous times, but all I have been able to accomplish is to get Shukrijumah's face featured one night on the show. And one night is just not enough! Glenn Beck, who has interviewed Hamid Mir on his TV show, has put Shukrijumah's mugshot on the show one time (but only mentioned one of his aliases, Jafer the Pilot, instead of naming all his aliases, including his real name, Adnan el-Shukrijumah). If we could get Shukrijumah's face on "America's Most Wanted" TV show for several weeks, and we told the American and Canadian people <u>why</u> were looking for him, that the FBI calls him "the next Mohammed Atta," the leader of Osama bin Laden's nuclear American Hiroshima attack, and America realizes the danger we're in, we could find him! Please, America, before it's too late!

I have often thought about having my friend Jerry Molen, who was the producer for sixteen of Steven Spielberg's films, including "Jurassic Park" and "Schindler's List," and who is very interested in counter-terrorism and homeland security issues, to ask his good friend Steven Spielberg, to do a movie called "The Hunt for Shukrijumah"! The only thing is we probably don't have time to make a movie to wake up America – the American Hiroshima is probably going to happen very, very soon!

Chapter Ten

What You Can Do to Help Stop the American Hiroshima, and How to Survive a Nuclear Attack

People often ask me what they can do to prevent this coming nuclear, biological, and chemical attack of Osama bin Laden, who is planning to "throw the kitchen sink at us" with everything he's got, including Mumbai-style assaults by jihadis with AK-47's, and Beslan-style attacks on our schools. I tell them, there are actually a lot of things just one individual can do to help stop this thing. You can call your two Senators and your Congressman and ask them to hold a Congressional hearing on Osama bin Laden's American Hiroshima plan for a nuclear attack on the United States. A Congressional Hearing would certainly get the media to do a full investigation of the evidence that suggests that al Qaeda is bringing a nuclear attack our way in the near future. And you can ask Congress to fund the development of the anti-radiation drug Neumune, that almost doubles the survival rate from radiation sickness.

Also, you can go to our website, www.afcpr.org (which stands for the American Foundation for Counter-Terrorism Policy and Research), and read the Must-Read Articles on the home page, and then email the homepage to all your friends, your Governor and Senators and Congressman, your newspaper, and any other media contacts you have. You can bring it up when you call in to your favorite talk radio show, and if they are skeptical and don't know what you're talking about, just give them the website www.afcpr.org, and if they go to that website, and see the home page, they will see exactly what you are talking about. You can make a donation to our non-profit foundation if you like, by hitting the donation button on the homepage of www.afcpr.org, and you can also make a donation to the Paul Williams Defense Fund by clicking on the donation button for his Defense Fund, or by going to paulwilliamsdefensefund.com.

You can call "America's Most Wanted" TV show at 1-800-CRIMETV, or 1-800-274-6388 and ask them to put Adnan Shukrijumah's face (the man the FBI calls "the next Mohammed Atta") on "America's Most Wanted" TV show. You can call the FBI 24 hour hotline at 202-324-3000 and ask them to see the website www.afcpr.org. You can go to the homepage of our website, www.afcpr.org, and see on the right-hand side of the homepage, a list of Action Items that you can do. And, most important of all, you can prepare your family for how to survive a nuclear attack.

Of course, if you are in the downtown area of one of the cities Osama has targeted for nuclear attack (New York, Washington, D.C., Philadelphia, Boston, Miami, Chicago, Houston, Los Angeles, Las Vegas, and Valdez, Alaska, the biggest oil terminal in the United States), you will be vaporized by the nuclear blast. However, if you live in the suburbs, you will survive the initial blast, and now it is very important that you know how to protect against deadly radiation sickness. Remember, many, many more people were killed from radiation than were killed from the initial blast in Hiroshima. In the suburbs, the radiation will subside very quickly, in three days decreasing to one hundredth of its initial strength. So stay in your homes, preferably in the basement if you have one, for three days. After three days, it is safe to take a ten minute trip outside once a day. After two weeks, you can go outside all the time. But if you go out of your home in the first three days, even just to pick up your child at school, if the wind is blowing the radioactive plume in your direction, both you and your child will get a fatal dose of radiation, and you will die a horrible death from radiation sickness over the next month or so.

If you don't have a basement, stay on the ground floor of your house, and build a make-shift shelter from up-turned couches, tables and the like, and huddle in it except for brief runs to the bathroom. This will provide more matter between you and the radioactivity outside. The radioactive dust from the fallout will cover your rooftop, your grass and trees and shrubbery, and your driveway. The radioactive dust, sometimes so fine when it has traveled hundreds of miles on the wind that you can not even see it, but it is still deadly, will emit deadly gamma rays that penetrate the walls of your house, but the walls, being matter, slow down the deadly rays. If you have a shelter of couches and upturned tables and the like, the matter will further slow down the gamma rays and make them harmless. Then, after three days, you can outside for a ten minute trip once a day, and after two weeks you can go outside all the time. Turn off your heat and air conditioning so the radioactive dust won't get inside the house, and shut all your windows and cover any cracks with duct tape. If you are outside, rush home, take off your clothes and leave them outside, and take a shower to get rid of the radioactive dust on your body. It is safe to drink water coming into your home through the pipes because water does not conduct radioactivity. But fill up your bathtubs with water, and use water sparingly, because if there is an EMP pulse, and it knocks out all the electricity, it may cause the water pumping stations to stop working.

Really, schools in the suburbs of the ten targeted cities should have a safety plan in place for what to do. The FBI and Homeland Security are so alarmed about this that they spent 400 million dollars developing nuclear radiation detectors they put around the mosques in the ten targeted cities, and in various traffic intersections or "choke-points" in Washington, D.C. and New York. But, as mentioned previously in this book, Steve Coll, noted counter-terrorism expert, wrote in the cover story of the March 12, 2007 New Yorker Magazine, that these nuclear radiation detectors cannot detect enriched uranium that is shielded in lead, and of course if the terrorists have a suitcase nuclear bomb they are going to have it in a lead container! We can detect plutonium through lead shielding, but not uranium. So if Homeland Security is so alarmed about the possibility of nuclear attack they spent 400 million dollars on nuclear radiation detectors (that don't even work if the bombs are shielded in lead!), why haven't they developed an effective plan to protect our kids if, God forbid, nuclear bombs are detonated by terrorists?

Schools should have a plan in place in the suburbs of these ten targeted cities (and perhaps in other cities as well, because we don't know if Osama has added to the target list in the six years that have passed since Khalid Sheikh Mohammed, who told us about them, was captured). If a nuclear blast happens downtown, the schools in the suburbs should keep the children in school, preferably in the basement if they have one, for three days until the radiation subsides enough to permit their parents to make a ten minute trip to pick them and get them back home, or wait for a week if the parent has a longer distance to go. There should be food and water on hand for three days at least and preferably two weeks.

Also, the schools should have on hand a supply of potassium iodide pills for the children, and any adults under age 40, to take to prevent thyroid cancer in the event of a nuclear blast. A nuclear blast creates radioactive iodine that can travel on the wind and cause thyroid cancer in people 300 miles away from the blast site. The body absorbs the radioactive iodine, which then accumulates in the thyroid gland, causing thyroid cancer in two years or less, especially in babies, children, teenagers, and young adults under the age of 40, since their thyroid glands are still developing. Thyroid cancer can easily be prevented simply by taking one potassium iodide pill per day for three days, or two weeks if you are in a very heavy radiation area. The iodide in the pills is absorbed by the body, and goes to the thyroid gland in the neck. When the radioactive iodine from the nuclear blast fallout enters the body, it goes to the thyroid gland, but since the thyroid gland is now totally full of good iodide, or iodine, the radioactive iodine is washed out of the body and does no harm. When the nuclear reactor at Chernobyl had its melt-down, releasing tons of radioactivity, the negligent government in the Ukraine did not give out any potassium iodide pills, and they ended up with 3,000 cases of thyroid cancer (and there were probably many more cases that the government did not report). The huge radioactive cloud blew on the wind directly over Poland. The government of Poland, however, did give out potassium iodide pills to its citizens, and they had zero cases of thyroid cancer! Potassium iodide pills make a huge difference!

Another important thing to do is to make sure you have at least three days supply of food and water in your home, and preferably have two months supply of food (even if you are not in a target city), and a big supply of water if you are in a target city, because the water pumping stations may be affected by the nuclear blast downtown. If you are not in a target city, you won't need a water supply, just a food supply, unless there is also an EMP attack, which would knock out electricity, causing pumping stations to malfunction. The reason why you need a two month food supply even if you are not in a target city, is because if Osama succeeds in his plan to destroy Houston, with all of its oil refineries, and Valdez, Alaska, the biggest oil terminal in the United States, where the oil tanker ships deliver oil from the Alaskan Pipeline to the U.S., there will be a nationwide shortage of gasoline for at least two months, and the big eighteen-wheeler trucks that bring food to all the cities in America will not be able to run. So you are going to need some canned goods!

What else are you going to need? You can order potassium iodide pills from the website www.ki4u.com (KI is the chemical symbol for potassium iodide) and the 4u means "for you." So www.ki4u.com means "potassium iodide for you"! (By the way, I want to make clear that I do not get money from any of the websites I mention, including my own website www.afcpr.org, which is a non-profit organization). You cannot get potassium iodide at drugstores – they just don't carry it. Some U.S. cities that are near nuclear reactors have a supply of potassium iodide pills, but really all cities should get a supply, especially the ten cities Osama has targeted. In the event of a nuclear blast, all the potassium iodide pills at www.ki4u.com will be quickly depleted, and you will not be able to get any, so it is important to order them now, while they are still available. You can order a small nuclear radiation detector that fits on a key chain and is about the size of a small whistle, so you can determine the level of radiation around the outside of your house, at www.nukalert.com, for a very reasonable price. And you can also get a small emergency radio which every family should have, in case the regular radio towers are knocked out by a nuclear blast or an EMP blast. You should have on hand a supply of cash, in case ATM's don't function. And you may need to get a gun and some ammo, in case there are food shortages and burglars try to steal your food. You can order food supplies, and other items, at www.survivormall.com.

I think it is shocking that the Department of Homeland Security has not told the American people what to do in the case of a nuclear blast. I guess they don't want to "alarm Americans," but as I have mentioned before, we Americans need to warned, and prepared, in case terrorists, both al Qaeda and Iran's Hezbollah (that according to FBI Director Robert Mueller are already here in the U.S.), succeed in their avowed goal of blowing up multiple American cities with nuclear bombs. I confronted the former Director of Homeland Security, Michael Chertoff (does this bring to mind Hurricane Katrina?) about the lack of preparation and warning the American people have been given, at an event at The Heritage Foundation (of which I was at the time a member of the foundation's President's Club). Michael Chertoff gave a speech on Homeland Security, and at the end of his speech he asked if there were any questions from the audience. I raised my hand, and was given the microphone to ask the first question. I explained how we had interviewed Hamid Mir, the Pakistani journalist who Osama bin Laden had told about the suitcase nukes he had acquired, and I asked what should people do in the event of a nuclear attack by terrorists, and shouldn't they stay inside for at least three days to avoid radiation sickness.

Michael Chertoff said, "The government will broadcast which way the radioactive plume is heading. However the radio and TV towers will probably be knocked out by the blast, so that is why everyone should have an emergency radio." I thought silently to myself, "That is great, Michael Chertoff, but I bet the 5 million people in the suburbs of Washington don't know they are supposed to have an emergency radio!" Then he went on to say, "And everyone should have at least a three-day supply of food in their homes." And again, I thought silently to myself, "That is great, Michael Chertoff, but I bet the 5 million people in the Washington suburbs don't know they are supposed to have at least a three day supply of food in their homes!" Then he said, "It's all on our website, www.ready. gov." Later, when I got home and looked up the website, I saw, after pages and pages of government gobbledygook, buried in the pages, was a one line sentence "everyone should get an emergency radio," not saying why people would need to get an emergency radio, like in the event of a terrorist nuclear attack, for instance. But I guess that might "unduly alarm Americans"! And buried on another page, is a one line sentence saying "Everyone should have at least a three day supply of food in their home." But again, it doesn't say why people should have at least a three day supply of food, like maybe so they can stay inside their homes for three days to avoid radiation sickness from a nuclear blast! I bet if people knew <u>why</u> Homeland Security was recommending everyone to have an emergency radio and three days supply of food in their home, because a nuclear attack by terrorists may happen soon, they would definitely get out and buy an emergency radio and three days supply of food! The event was filmed by CNN, and I gave the CNN reporter our info after the event was over.

We are not being adequately warned by our Homeland Security Department!!! Michael Chertoff should have, and now that he is no longer Director of Homeland Security, the present Director, Janet Napolitano, should get on ABC, CBS, NBC, CNN, and FOX News, and tell everyone in the country to get an emergency radio and at least three days supply of food, or really, two months supply of food and tell them why, "in the event of a nuclear attack by terrorists" to really get people's attention so they will know it is a real danger and prepare accordingly. Oh, but I forgot – the government says we are no longer in a "War on Terror"! The War on Terror is over, they say. And we are not to use the inflammatory term "Islamic radical terrorist" or "jihadi terrorist"! Unfortunately, we are about to find out that although we have stopped fighting "the War on Terror," or, as it is more correctly termed, "the War Against Global Islamo-Facism," our Islamic radical extremist enemies, sponsored by terrorist-supporting states like Iran and Syria, and radical elements in Saudi Arabia and other Muslim countries, are very much at war with us, and as they scream "Death to America," their plans to actually bring "Death to America" are about to come to fruition, as Osama bin Laden and Iran's American Hiroshima attack draws closer and closer.

You can go to www.ki4u.com not only to get your potassium iodide pills, but the website also has a great eleven page guide for how to survive a nuclear blast, titled "What to Do If a Nuclear Disaster is Imminent." You can see the same guide on our website, www.afcpr.org. Everyone should read this guide to survival. You can go to www.spike.com/full-episode/nuclear-attack/34350 to see a great video on how to survive a nuclear attack. You can order copies of this book you presently have in your hand, <u>The American Hiroshima: Osama's Plan for a Nuclear Attack, and One Man's Attempt to Warn America</u>, at Barnes and Noble, iUniverse. com, or Amazon.com, or any bookseller (if it's not on the shelf, you can order it), and you can give copies to your friends and family and media people and government officials and your political representatives. You can do your part to encourage investigation of this most serious matter, and you can prepare your family for survival. You can vote for political candidates who will enact a Pro-Life Amendment and a Pro-Marriage Amendment to the Constitution, and get America back to God and His protection. And you can pray America will heed the words of God, who says in 2 Chronicles 7:14, "If my people, which are called by my name, shall humble themselves, and pray, and seek my face, and turn from their wicked ways: then will I hear from heaven, and will forgive their sin, and will heal their land."

God bless you all, God bless America, and America, bless God!

Epilogue

Some people would ask, "If Osama is going to blow up ten American cities when Israel attacks Iran's nuclear sites, shouldn't we stop Israel from attacking Iran?" I think we must stop Iran from getting nukes, at all cost, and allow, or even assist Israel to take out Iran's nuclear sites, because if Iran does get nukes, it will give them to Osama and other terrorists, and instead of just ten American cities being blown up, it will be 50 to 100 American cities! We must stop Iran from getting nuclear weapons!

So why hasn't Osama attacked already, if he has functional nuclear devices in ten cities in America? This is the question many people ask, including Fred Barnes of Fox News and the Weekly Standard, who moderated a debate I sponsored at the National Press Club in Washington, D.C., between Dr. Paul Williams, author of <u>Osama's Revenge: The Next 9/11</u>, arguing that Osama has suitcase nukes that could already be in the country, and Richard Miniter, author of <u>Disinformation</u>, arguing that suitcase nukes are an urban myth. The thinking goes: If Osama bin Laden got hold of a nuclear bomb, he would use it as fast as he could, before the FBI or CIA could catch him and stop him. While it is true that Osama was very nervous about the 9/11 plot being found out (he wanted Mohammed Atta to do the attack about five or six weeks earlier, but Atta insisted on needing more time to train the muscle hijackers), he apparently has found a way to avoid having to be worried about discovery of his plan, and having to rush to do the attack before it can be discovered.

Rakan Ben Williams, an English convert to Islam and an al Qaeda commander, suggests that Al Qaeda has a fail-safe type of plan, so that if our intelligence agencies were to discover the plot, it would just make it go off sooner. For example, if the FBI were to discover one suitcase nuclear device in a city, the terrorist plotters in the other 9 targeted cities would then go ahead and detonate their nuclear devices. Rakan Ben Williams writes to the American people, "Let me inform you about your inability to stop them [the nuclear attacks] before they are carried out. The best you could do would be to accelerate the day of carrying out the operations. In other words, if we schedule the operation to take place tomorrow, the best you could do is to make it happen today." He goes on to say, "I will not give you any more clues; this is enough as a wake-up call. Perhaps the American people will start thinking about the magnitude of the danger that is coming their way."[30] Osama bin Laden is a very capable and patient planner, an evil genius, as evidenced by his effectiveness in bringing down the World Trade Center Towers, and destroying part of the Pentagon, an operation, as he calls it, that took him five years to plan and execute. And he has been planning and working on his American Hiroshima plan for much longer, ever since his first attempts to find enriched uranium in 1992! He will not pull the trigger on the American Hiroshima, the Grand Finale and crowning achievement of his life's work, until every preparation is made, every aspect is firmly in place, and world events bring about a galvanizing event, as Paul Williams says, like Israel or the U.S. attacking Iran's nuclear sites (which could happen by the end of this year, or sooner). If Israel or the U.S. attacks Iran, Taliban chieftains have told Hamid Mir that Osama, aided and abetted by Iran, will then attack America. This way, Osama thinks he will get approval from the Islamic ummah or Muslim world, for killing millions of infidel Americans and ushering in the Day of Islam where the great Mahdi (the Twelfth Imam) will come and establish a world-wide Muslim Caliphate which will rule the world. If Osama killed ten million Americans with nuclear weapons now, he might get some disapproval from Muslims for such a wholesale relatively unprovoked slaughter, but if he waits until Israel or the U.S. strikes Iran, he thinks it will be seen as justified for him to retaliate.

Also there is some evidence that Iran is sheltering Osama, keeping him in safe houses in Iran (that may be why we cannot seem to locate bin Laden in Afghanistan or Pakistan, because he may well be in Iran), and Iran does not want Osama to attack America prematurely, because then America, if ten of its cities go up in mushroom clouds may retaliate with a nuclear attack on Iran, if America (correctly) realizes that Iran assisted Osama to weaponize fissionable material (enriched uranium), as British Intelligence MI6 has discovered as early as 2006. Iran would rather wait, and get more time to develop their nuclear arsenal; however, if Israel or the United States were to attack and destroy Iran's nuclear sites, then Iran may feel it has nothing left to lose, and may tell Osama to go ahead with the American Hiroshima attack, and Iran will put the blame on Osama. So all of this may explain why Osama has not yet done his American Hiroshima attack.

Although Richard Miniter would like to believe suitcase nukes are an urban myth, unfortunately they are very real, as Parade magazine (the most widely read publication in the world, by the way) reported.[31] The Soviet Union made over a hundred of them for the KGB, of which at least 80 have gone missing after the chaotic break-up of the Soviet Union, and cannot be accounted for, according to high ranking Russian officials.[32]The United States made a large number of small tactical nuclear weapons of one to ten kiloton yield (SADMs, or Small Atomic Demolition Munitions), such as the Davy Crocket rucksack nuclear bomb that could be carried in a backpack. Also, as Congressman Curt Weldon demonstrated with a mock-up of a suitcase nuclear bomb to Congress, suitcase bombs can also be made from nuclear artillery shells, which the United States and the Soviet Union had hundreds of, with a one to ten kiloton explosive yield (for comparison, the bomb that was dropped on Hiroshima had a thirteen kiloton yield). To pretend that there is no such thing as a suitcase nuclear bomb, and that those bombs could never get in the hands of terrorists, is psychological denial to the worst degree. The situation in the former Soviet Union was very very chaotic after it broke up, and Soviet nuclear weapons and nuclear materials were not secured well at all, and it is very possible nuclear weapons were stolen and sold on the black market to Osama bin Laden, as he and Ayman al-Zawahiri told Hamid Mir.

And although it would take technically skilled people to hotwire suitcase nukes so that they could be detonated without a code from Moscow, as Yossef Bodansky, former Director of Congress' Task Force on Terrorism for 16 years, writes in his book Chechen Jihad, Osama hired former Soviet SPESNAZ Special Forces soldiers whose job it had been to maintain the suitcase nukes for the KGB, to hotwire the bombs so they can be detonated by a terrorist. And yes, the bombs have to be maintained and serviced about every six months, but, according to Hamid Mir and others, Osama has a lot of nuclear technicians (Adnan Shukrijumah and his accomplices) to maintain the nukes for him. And there is evidence Osama has obtained other nuclear weapons on the black market, and has also gotten help in weaponizing enriched uranium (fissionable material) he has obtained on the black market, from rogue Pakistani nuclear scientists who helped A.Q. Khan develop Pakistan's nuclear bomb, who are now also helping Iran develop its nuclear bomb. So to think Osama bin Laden has not acquired nuclear weapons is, unfortunately, just wishful thinking!

One of the most sophisticated, and intelligent efforts to try to show that Osama has not acquired nuclear weapons is the book Will Terrorists Go Nuclear by Brian Michael Jenkins. I have very carefully and thoroughly examined every one of his arguments, because I would very much like to think that Osama does not have nuclear capability, and is not going to destroy ten American cities in a nuclear attack! Unfortunately, I must tell you, every one of his arguments, although appearing plausible at first glance, have flaws, and, to the observer experienced in the counter-terrorism research relating to the issue of al Qaeda's quest for nuclear weapons, upon further analysis are seen to be incorrect. I do not have time in this book to go through each one of his claims and show the subtle errors in his logic. But to help you perhaps understand an important reason to doubt Brian Michael Jenkins' assertions, well meaning though they are, in their (futile) attempt to try to reassure us that Osama does not have nuclear weapons and we don't have to worry about a nuclear attack on America, it suffices to say that Brian Michael Jenkins was the person who, before 9/11, asserted that Osama bin Laden would never carry out a mass murder attack on America, because he would not want to alienate people from his cause. Of course, 9/11 showed that Osama certainly would carry out a mass murder attack, and in the fatwa he obtained, Osama intends to carry out a much larger mass murder attack in his coming American Hiroshima, in which he hopes to, as the fatwa says, kill ten million Americans with nuclear weapons, three million of which need to be children to achieve parity for Muslim children Osama believes have been killed by America and Israel.

I sincerely hope and pray we are wrong. I pray to God that we are wrong, that Osama does not have functional nuclear weapons here in the United States. If he does have them, I pray they will be duds, that perhaps they were not properly maintained. If they are functional, I pray that our FBI and CIA and the other Intelligence Agencies and law enforcement agencies in America will find them in time, and defuse them. But it certainly would make me feel better if we could get this issue out into the media, and warn the American people! If the media would fully investigate it, and if the American people were told about it so they could look for the bombs and the terrorists, especially if we could get Adnan Shukrijumah's face on America's Most Wanted TV show, we might could stop this truly catastrophic, horrible attack that is coming. And if we could not stop it, we could at least tell people how to avoid deadly radiation sickness, and millions of lives could be saved. Please pray with us that God will help us, and let's get close to God and His protection, and let's stop Osama bin Laden's and Iran's American Hiroshima attack! Again as God says in the Bible, in 2 Chronicles 7:14, "If my people, which are called by my name, shall humble themselves, and pray, and seek my face, and turn from their wicked ways; then will I hear from heaven, and will forgive their sin, and will heal their land." Let's listen to God!

Appendix First Article

Osama bin Laden Plans US Attack That Will 'Outdo' September 11

Warning of new bin Laden attack

OSAMA bin Laden is planning an attack against the United States that will "outdo by far" September 11, an Arab newspaper in London has reported. bin Laden 'planning US attack'

Goal to 'outdo' September 11, al-Qaeda reinforces training camps.

And according to a former senior Yemeni al-Qaeda operative, the terrorist organization has entered a "positive phase", reinforcing specific training camps around the world that will lead the next "wave of action" against the West.

The warning, on the front page of an Arabic newspaper published in London, Al-Quds Al-Arabi and widely reported in the major Italian papers - quotes a person described as being "very close to al-Qaeda" in Yemen.

The paper is edited by Abdel al-Bari Atwan, who has interviewed Osama in the past. Suggest in one report that, bin Laden is himself closely following preparations for an attack against the US and aims to "change the face of world politics and economics".

The ex-operative says he remains in contact with current chiefs of the organization in Yemen and that only six months ago bin Laden had sent a message to all jihad cells in the Arab world which asked them not to interact with their governments or local political parties and to deny any request for mediation or formal talks.

The source also said that during the next few days the terrorist organization may send a sign of its violent intentions.

The warning has emerged at the same time as publication of a report leaked to The Telegraph newspaper which reveals that a document drawn up by the intelligence branch of the Ministry of Defense says that thousands of extremists are active in the UK. believed to have been trained in overseas terrorist camps.

Security officials, The Telegraph reports, are convinced al-Qaeda cells will attempt another "spectacular" inside the UK with major transport centres, such as airports and train stations, the most likely targets. Other targets include the Houses of Parliament, Whitehall and Buckingham and St James' palaces, with the threat level described as "severe".

Appendix Second Article

FROM JOSEPH FARAH'S G2 BULLETIN

Brit MI6 confirms bin Laden nukes

Pakistani scientists reportedly advising al-Qaida on weaponization of uranium it has obtained

Posted: May 07, 2006

1:00 AM Eastern

WorldNetDaily.com

Editor's note: The following story is adapted from Joseph Farah's G2 Bulletin, the premium, online intelligence newsletter published by the founder of WND. Annual subscriptions are now available at the discounted price of $99 a year, which includes a free copy of Farah's latest book, "Taking America Back." Monthly subscriptions are also available to credit card users for just $9.95.

MI6, Britain's secret intelligence service, has identified six Pakistani scientists working in Iran's nuclear bomb program who have been "advising al-Qaida on how to weaponize fissionable materials it has now obtained."

MI6 and the International Atomic Energy Agency believe the scientists have played a major role enabling Iran to be "well advanced in providing uranium enriched materials for nuclear bombs," reported Alexander Cirilovic, a nuclear terrorism expert in Paris.

Both high-level MI6 and CIA sources have confirmed the scientists would only have been allowed to assist al-Qaida with the authority of Iran's unpredictable President Mahmoud Ahmadinejad.

The revelation comes at a time when Washington has increased pressure on Tehran to give up its nuclear weapons program.

The scientists worked for Dr. A.Q. Khan, the "father of the Islamic bomb," who is now under house arrest in Pakistan after confessing he had provided both Iran and North Korea with details of how make their own nuclear bombs.

The MI6 report to other intelligence services followed bin Laden's recent threats to unleash a new wave of terror - with Britain and the United States his prime targets.

Recently, from his lair in north Pakistan, bin Laden boasted that "al-Qaida did not find it difficult to obtain the weapons grade material. We have contacts in Russia with other militant groups. Enough material to make a tactical nuke is available for $15 million dollars."

Former CIA operative David Dastych, a G2B contributor from Poland and one of the agency's experts on nuclear terrorism, said: "The traffic in nuclear materials is ongoing and growing."

Bin Laden's material is hidden somewhere in the mountain fastness between Iran and Afghanistan.

Its proximity to Iran's own nuclear facilities has made it easy for the Pakistani scientists to assist al-Qaida.

Like Khan, all are strong al-Qaida supporters. One, Bashiruddin Mahmood, was briefly arrested in 2004 by the Pakistan Intelligence service.

He said he had met the Taliban leader Mullah Omar and a high-ranking al-Qaida operative.

In his statement Mahmood admitted: "They had asked me to devise a radiological bomb. It would be constructed from nuclear material wrapped in conventional high explosive which bin Laden had obtained from a nuclear storage site in Uzbekistan. "I refused to do so."

Despite a CIA request to have him transferred to the United States for further questioning, Mahmood was set free. Shortly afterward he fled from Pakistan to Iran.

With him went five other senior scientists at the Khan laboratories. They were Muhammad Zubair, Saeed Akhhter, Murad Qasim, Imtaz Baig and Waheed Nasir.

They had helped Khan to successfully detonate Pakistan's first nuclear bomb at a test site beneath the Baluchistan desert.

"Depending on the quality of the fissionable material bin Laden has obtained, the combined scientific skills would be able to create considerably more than a "dirty bomb," said Cirilovic.

This article was written by Gordon Thomas, an Irish journalist specializing in international intelligence matters and a regular contributor to Joseph Farah's G2 Bulletin.

Appendix Third Article

Ryan Mauro's Interview with Hamid Mir in WorldTheats.com

AI-Qaeda's Hidden Arsenal and Sponsors: Interview with Hamid Mir

Hamid Mir truly has deep access inside AI-Qaeda and the Taliban. He is best known as the last journalist to interview Osama Bin Laden, and the only one to do so after the attacks of September 11, 2001. He is currently the Bureau Chief of Islamabad for Geo TV and is writing a biography on Osama Bin Laden. He has interviewed countless members of AI-Qaeda and the Taliban in many countries over the years.

Mir has had remarkable reliability. For example, most recently he said that Osama Bin Laden was going to issue a new tape, but the mainstream media did not report it. A few days later, a tape was released. He was the only one to predict the event.

RM: What governments have sponsored AI-Qaeda and Osama Bin Laden over the years?

HM: I think it was the Taliban government which sponsored AI- Qaeda from 1996 to 2001. In between, the U.S. government engaged the Taliban in talks, some of which were arranged by Pakistan. Islamabad and Washington started covert operations against AI-Qaeda in 1999 (under Clinton and Nawaz Sharif) but they failed. After 9/11, it is the present Iranian regime which is secretly helping AI-Qaeda because the U.S. is supporting Israel openly.

RM: What governments have been friendly to AI-Qaeda in the past? Where/are there links between AI-Qaeda and Iraq, Syria, North Korea, etc?

HM: I don't think that Iraq had any direct link with AI-Qaeda. Saddam tried to contact Osama Bin Laden in 1998 but he was not entertained. Syria is a safe haven for AI-Qaeda now but the Syrian government is not trusted by the AI-Qaeda commanders in Iraq. I will not comment on North Korea. This is a point on which I am still not clear and am still trying to investigate.

RM: Can you give us some detail about the Russians advisors you said were helping the Taliban? Why would the Russians help them? What are they helping them with? And how long; if Russia has provided assistance to radical Islamic movements like al-Qaeda?

HM: What I said was that Russia is covertly supporting Taliban insurgents in Afghanistan. The spokesman of the Afghan Interior Ministry, Lutaffulah Mashal, told me in September 2005 in Kabul that the Taliban are getting modem Russian-made weapons. He suspected that Russia may be taking revenge on the U.S. for supporting the Afghan Mujahedeen against Russia in the 1980s.

I met a Taliban commander in Ghazi last year who showed me a small mobile phone bomb. He said that they will use that bomb against the British troops very soon in southern Afghanistan. How can they make mobile phone bombs on their own? The Taliban are receiving weapons from AI-Qaeda also, which are being smuggled in from Iran.

RM: tt has been reported that you believe AI-Qaeda has nuclear weapons. How did you come up with this conclusion?

HM: I came up with this conclusion after eight years of investigation and research in the remote mountain areas of Afghanistan and Pakistan. I travelled to Iraq, Iran, Sudan, Syria, Uzbekistan, and Russia and met dozens of people. I interviewed not only AI-Qaeda operatives but met scientists and top U.S. officials also. I will have the details in my coming book.

At least two AI-Qaeda operatives claimed that the organization smuggled suitcase nukes inside America. But I have no details on who did it. But I do have details about who smuggled uranium inside America and how.

I am very careful when speaking about AI-Qaeda's nuclear capabilities. I've met many people in AI-Qaeda who have claimed that uranium and nuclear bombs were smuggled to

94

America, and I'll quote them in my book. However, when I speak for myself, I don't rely on claims by AI-Qaeda. I rely upon my own investigations.

RM: What's the name of your book? Will new details and proof of AI-Qaeda's acquisition of nukes be presented?

MM: My publisher has not authorized me to disclose the name of the book, but it will be a biography of Osama Bin Laden in which I will disclose his future plans and details of his nuclear designs. The world will come to know that which is the real AI-Qaeda.

RM: How many nuclear weapons does AI-Qaeda possess?

HM: As far as I know, they smuggled three suitcase nukes from Russia to Europe. They smuggled many kilos of enriched uranium inside America for their dirty bomb projects. They said in 1999 that they must have material for more than six dirty bombs in America. They tested at least one dirty bomb in the Kunar province of Afghanistan in 2000.

They have planned an attack bigger than 9/11, even before 9/11 happened. Osama Bin Laden trained 42 fighters to destroy the American economy and military might. 19 were used on 9/11, 23 are still "sleeping" inside America waiting for a wake-up call from Bin Laden.

RM: If AI-Qaeda has tactical suitcase nukes, not Just "dirty bombs," why would they deploy them to Europe instead of the United States?

HM: Actually, I lost track of the three suitcase nukes after they were smuggled into Italy. I tried my best to get more information about those bombs but I am only one man. I only received one tip that Chechen members of AI-Qaeda wanted to smuggle one bomb into London, one into Paris, and one into California, but some dispute developed with the Italian underworld over the method of payment. This was in the year 2000.

RM: Were actual tactical nukes deployed to the US? And is the leader of the nuclear plot Adnan el-Shukrijumah as believed by some experts?

HM: AI-Qaeda leaders claimed to have deployed their tactical weapons inside America. But when I tried to track the transportation of those weapons from Georgia, I lost track in Italy. I don't know the location of these today because my source left Afghanistan for Iraq last year. On the other hand, they claimed to me that weapons were smuggled to America through Mexico.

According to my notes, the man responsible for organizing the nuclear attacks inside America is not Adnan but is Muhammad Sher Khan, but this may be an alias for Adnan.

RM: When is your book coming out?

HM: I am just putting on some finishing touches to the manuscript. I am planning to publish the book this year. I am going to reveal the secret world of Osama Bin Laden through my own eyes. I don't think it would be difficult for you to understand that writing some facts about Osama Bin Laden is not an easy job in Muslim countries today.

Yes, our governments are against him but he is popular among the masses. Common Muslims do not believe he is responsible for the 9/11 attacks, and I am going to write about how 9/11 was planned and implemented by Osama Bin Laden. What happened to Osama Bin Laden after 9/11? How did he escape from Tora Bora? Where has he spent his last four years? Where and how did he organize the new insurgency in Afghanistan and Iraq? (think I will face a lot of criticism for my Iran/AI-Qaeda chapter from the Muslim media. I am going to reveal facts that nobody can deny. I am very careful. I wrote each and every word only after many cross-checks. I even cross-checked the claims made by Osama Bin Laden. I will definitely raise some issues like why he is still at large, and I'll have to talk about the weaknesses of the Pakistani and American secret services. I will not enjoy the publication of my book because I do not live in an ideal democracy. I am not bothered by who might benefit from my research. I have only one objective in mind; to keep the historical record straight.

RM: How can you be positive that the Information regarding AI-Qaeda's nuclear capabilities isn't disinformation meant to frighten their enemies?

HM: That was the argument many U.S. experts presented in 1998 when Osama Bin Laden declared war on the U.S. Don't underestimate your enemy. You may dislike them but they don't lie, They may give a deadline to Muslims sometime to leave America and then they will attack. That is what was discussed in one of the AI-Qaeda meetings in Kunar in 2003.

RM: In a recent interview, you described a nuclear test in Kunar province in the year 2000 where an Egyptian scientist lost an eye. Was it a radiological "dirty bomb" or a more serious tactical nuclear weapon?

HM: It was a radiological dirty bomb.

RM: You have said that you think AI-Qaeda may use the nukes once Iran is bombed by the U.S. Is that your opinion or is this what you've been told?

MM: This is my opinion. No AI-Qaeda leader has ever admitted that they are working with Iran. I also think that, maybe, the Iranians will organize some attacks inside America and you will accuse AI- Qaeda.

RM: Do you know when AI-Qaeda's nuclear weapons were forward deployed?

HM: I think they transferred their materials inside America between 1999 and 2001, before September the 11th.

RM: Why hasn't AI-Qaeda used nuclear weapons if they possess them?

HM: They are waiting for the proper time. They want the U.S. to be involved in a mass killing of Muslims, so that they will have some justification. That is what I was told by a top AI-Qaeda leader in the Kunar Mountains of Afghanistan.

RM: Where did AI-Qaeda get the training to handle and detonate nuclear weapons? Some experts believe that Soviet- era nukes have sufficient security measures to stop their unauthorized use.

HM: They trained dozens of boys who can make dirty bombs by purchasing material from some medical stores and then they will detonate these materials with some uranium from X-Ray machines. They are not just dependent on Soviet nukes.

RM: How would AI-Qaeda be able to defeat American capabilities to detect the nuclear weapons? Are they disguised?

HM: I think that these materials are disguised. The U.S. needs some political strategy to address this issue. It is not only the U.S. but many European countries that are the targets of AI-Qaeda's nuclear attacks. The world is not safe. An attack in California or London will not affect only the West, but it will affect the whole Muslim world.

There needs to be a well-coordinated effort to make the world safe. I am very much concerned because I have a lot of friends in America. I like common Americans. They are a good and frank people. Why should they pay the price of their government's bad policies? We have to move to stop both AI-Qaeda and Bush.

RM: The Muslim world was in an uproar after the US invaded Iraq. Why wasn't that viewed as appropriate justification?

HM: Saddam Hussein was not popular in the Muslim world. Osama hated him. Iran hated him. He was once considered an American agent. The majority of Muslims were initially happy that Saddam was dislodged, but then anger spread against the U.S. after the Abu Ghraib jail scandal. Now Muslims think that America invaded Iraq for oil, not for WMDs. Where are the WMDs? America must answer this question NOW.

RM: Does Al-Qaeda possess advanced chemical and biological weapons?

HM: They can make anthrax but they don't have advanced biological weapons. Their plus point is their suicide bombers. They have planned nuclear and biological attacks using suicide bombers.

Posted by Ryan Mauro at 10:58 am

Appendix Fourth Article-
Osama's Coming Attack: An American Hiroshima?

I.   Osama warns America in his January 19, 2006 audiotape, "The operations are under preparation and you will see them in your homes the minute the preparations are through."

He offers a truce to America, just as he did to England and Europe, 14 months before the London 7/7 bombings. Ayman al-Zawahiri and Adam Gadahn, the American Al Qaeda, appear soon after in a videotape urging Americans to convert to Islam. Then Ayman al-Zawahiri says "Now we have fulfilled all the requirements of Islamic law - Osama has given you many warnings, he has offered you a truce, and he has given you the chance to convert to Islam. Now we are justified in attacking you."

II.   Christianne Amanpour, in the CNN TV documentary "In the Footsteps of Bin Laden," points out:

1.   Osama warned 3 weeks before 9/11 in the AI-Quds al-Arabi newspaper that he was going to "attack America in an unprecedented way for its support of Israel." When Osama says he is going to do something he does it.

2.   Osama took it to heart when some Muslim scholars criticized him after 9/11 for not following Islam's law and offering his enemy a chance for a truce before striking them. He then offered England and Europe a truce - when they rejected it, he did the London bombings. Now he has offered America a truce,

3.   Before he did 9/11, Osama got a fatwa saying it was okay to kill civilians. Now he has gotten a fatwa saying it is okay to kill 10 million Americans with nuclear weapons. Guess what is going to happen next?

III.   Hamid Mir, the Pakistani journalist who has interviewed Osama three times, was summoned to Afghanistan on September 12, 2006 for an interview with the top Al Qaeda commander in Afghanistan, Abu Dawood. Abu Dawood said "tell all the Muslims they must leave America now, especially New York and Washington, because Osama has completed his cycle of warnings, his preparations are through and he may attack America at any time. This is their last warning."

IV.   The American Hiroshima:

1.   Osama has been working on his American Hiroshima plan since 1993. He has obtained "suitcase nukes" - some are the size of suitcases, some are the size of refrigerators - during the breakup of the former Soviet Union. He has obtained uranium and cesium from other sources (in 2001, a lead-lined container of uranium worth millions on the black market was found left behind in the tunnels of Kandahar after Al Qaeda fled in haste). Hans Blix, the former U.N. Weapons Inspector for the IAEA, reported to the U.N. in 2004 that Osama did indeed obtain 20 suitcase nuclear bombs, Han Blix interviewed the Russian officials who reported the theft of the bombs, and he also interviewed the Chechen Muslim rebels who witnessed the sale of the bombs to Osama. This was reported by the BBC, the London Times, and several Arabic newspapers, and is verified by the intelligence services of the U.S., Pakistan, Britain, and Russia. Yossef Bodansky, the director of the Congressional Task Force on Terrorism from 1988-1998, told a Congressional Committee that Osama has obtained nuclear weapons. Bodansky also says, "Osama has recruited former Soviet Special Forces SPETSNAZ soldiers to teach Al Qaeda how to maintain and operate the bombs".

V.   Adnan Shukrijumah, who the FBI calls "The Next Mohammed Atta" enlists the aid of Mara Salvatrucha (MS13), the Latino Gang that smuggles cocaine, heroin, and humans through the Mexican border into the U.S., to smuggle the suitcase nukes into 10 cities in America. (see the website WWW.STOPDOOMSDAY.COM).

VI.   Other evidence that terrorists have obtained and are actively seeking to obtain nuclear weapons - in October 2001, Israeli soldiers stop a terrorist attempting to cross the Allenby Bridge on his way to the Ramallah checkpoint with a nuclear device roughly the size of a small refrigerator in his van. It is a plutonium implosion nuclear bomb. This is verified by Mossad, and also by Richard Sale, a journalist who works with the CIA. Major General

Robert Patterson, father of Colonel "Buzz" Patterson, who was in charge of securing our borders for the military in the early 1990's, said in 1992 he was directly involved in stopping a terrorist who attempted to bring a nuclear device into the U.S., and he also said he had heard of two other such cases . Since 2002, authorities have thwarted 300 attempts by terrorists around the world to illegally obtain "dangerous nuclear materials" that could make a "dirty bomb."

VII.   Hamid Mir tells us Osama has smuggled suitcase nuclear bombs into cities in Europe and also through the porous Mexican border into cities in America. Kahlid Shaikh Mohammed, the mastermind of 9/11, says Osama is going to unleash a "nuclear hellstorm" on America. Sharif al-Masri, captured Al Qaeda leader, said 2 years ago that Osama was planning to forward deploy nuclear devices through Mexico into America. Osama himself and Ayman al- Zawahiri told Hamid Mir they have acquired suitcases nukes.

VIII.   A possible nerve center for the American Hiroshima - Dr. Paul Williams believes one of the nerve centers for the American Hiroshima plan could be McMaster University in Hamilton, Ontario, Canada. It is there, at McMaster, that Adnan Shukrijumah is alleged to have stolen 180 pounds of nuclear material in 2002. The FBI verifies that Shukrijumah and other known terrorists were spotted in Hamilton in 2002. Dr. Williams believes that there could be many Jihadi Islamic students and professors at McMaster. Dr. Williams believes it is possible that some students are taught nuclear technology so they can service and maintain the suitcase nukes which may already be in 10 American cities, possibly hidden in mosques of those cities.

McMaster University has sued Dr. Williams for saying Shukrijumah may have stolen 180 pounds of nuclear material, even though Bill Gertz of the Washington Times, John Loftus of WABC, and others have written about it. McMaster offered to drop the lawsuit if Dr. Williams would retract his statement, but Dr. Williams refuses to back down. Instead, he welcomes the lawsuit because it will now allow him to search all of McMaster's records through the legal process of discovery. Dr. Williams believes if he can expose one of the possible nerve centers for the American Hiroshima plan, which he believes could be the nexus of Islamic professors and students who give and receive training in nuclear technology at the research nuclear reactor at McMaster, he can possibly stop Osama's American Hiroshima plan from happening. To help Dr. Williams stop the American Hiroshima, please go to the website www.paulwilliamsdefensefund.com and donate to his legal defense fund. and please check out www.stopdoomsday. com and www.AFCPR. Org, for further information about the American Hiroshima.

Appendix Fifth Article

Dr. Cort's 2008 Presidential Campaign Speech to the Iowa Christian Alliance

To the Christians of the Iowa Christian Alliance, and Christians everywhere, Greetings in the name of our Lord and Savior Jesus Christ! I greatly look forward to meeting you all at the House Party you are giving me in Des Moines at 6:30 PM on Thursday, August 2. I appreciate all that you have done for the Christian cause. God is working through us, and His purposes will be fulfilled!

Let me tell you a little about myself. I am a Christian psychiatrist from Birmingham, Alabama. I was living a very happy and contented life as a psychiatrist when 9/11 happened. I was horrified, as were we all. I decided to see if I could help prevent such a terrible disaster from ever happening again. I began to attend counter-terrorism conferences around the country, such as The Intelligence Summit (see www.intelligencesummit.org) and other conferences. The Lord blessed me by having me meet many intelligence experts from around the world, such as General Tom McInerney, Fox News and CNN military analyst, General Paul Vallely, Fox News and CNN military analyst, Yossef Bodansky, who directed the Congressional Task Force on Terrorism for 16 years, Fred Barnes, editor of The Weekly Standard, and co-host of Fox News "The Beltway Boys", Dr. Paul Williams, author of the best seller Osama's Revenge: The Next 9/11 and four other books about Osama bin Laden's "American Hiroshima" plan to blow up ten American cities (the most recent book the widely acclaimed Day of Islam), John Loftus, President of The Intelligence Summit, and many others.

I wrote a book about 9/11, and over the next five years the Lord lead me on many counter-terrorism investigations with a true genius, Dr. Paul Williams, who I think of as Sherlock Holmes, while I am the humble Dr. Watson!

In the course of our investigations, we interviewed Hamid Mir, the top Pakistani journalist, who interviews Tony Blair and Condoleeza Rice when they go to Pakistan. Hamid Mir has interviewed Osama bin Laden three times, and he is the only person who has interviewed Osama after 9/11. Hamid confirmed what we had already learned from several other reliable sources, that Osama bin Laden has a plan he calls "The American Hiroshima" where he blows up 7 to 10 American cities with suitcase nuclear bombs, and that there is a lot of evidence that he has already smuggled these bombs into America through the porous Mexican border. We had already learned from Yossef Bodansky that Osama had acquired 20 suitcase nuclear bombs when the Soviet Union broke up, and that he had hired 20 former Russian SPETZNAZ soldiers, whose job it had been to maintain and service suitcase nukes for the KGB, to help Osama maintain and service his suitcase nukes (you can learn more about this on our counter-terrorism websites www.afcpr.org and www.stopdoomsday.com). And we knew that when Khalid Sheik Mohammed, Osama's master planner for 9/11, was captured, he told the CIA (and this was on his computer as well) that Osama was planning a "nuclear hellstorm for America" and that 7 cities, including Washington and New York, were targeted, with three alternate cities which may be added. And, in former CIA Director George Tenet's new book, he says that some of the Pakistani nuclear scientists who helped A. Q. Khan develop Pakistan's nuclear bomb, were also helping Osama with his nuclear program. And in NewsMax.com Chris Ruddy's recent interview with FBI Director Robert Mueller, Mueller confirms that Osama wants to blow up Washington and New York and is "desperately seeking nuclear materials" and Mueller often can't sleep at night for worrying about it.

Then, in September, Hamid Mir told me and Dr. Williams that he had been summoned to Afghanistan for an interview with the top Al Qaeda commander in Afghanistan, Abu Dawood, who said, "Hamid Mir, tell all the Muslims in America they need to leave now, especially New York and Washington, because Osama has completed his cycle of warnings, his preparations are through, and he may attack America at any time; he does not want to hurt the Muslims, but if they do not leave he doesn't have any other choice, and this is their last warning".

Dr. Williams and I have been to the FBI several times with our information, but unfortunately the FBI is dropping the ball on Osama's "American Hiroshima" plan just like they dropped the ball on 9/11. I used to think the FBI was really sharp and on top of things until the trial of Zacarias Moussaoui (Moussaoui was the "twentieth hijacker" who was captured a month before 9/11). At the trial in New York City it came out that the field FBI agent wanted to search Moussaoui's computer (remember, Moussaoui had terrorist ties, and wanted to learn to fly airplanes in midair but did not care about learning to land or take off), and the field officer requested his bureaucrat superiors at the FBI to get him a search warrant to search Moussaoui's computer, but they turned him down. He knew this was vital, so he tried again and again, but they turned him down again and again. In fact, he tried 70 times in the month before 9/11 to get a search warrant to search Moussaoui's computer, and 70 times he was turned down by his FBI superiors. And then 9/11 happened, and there was a good chance if they had searched Moussaoui's computer they may have found evidence to help stop 9/11!

So the FBI is not the all-powerful agency I had once thought it was, and unfortunately they are failing to stop Osama's "American Hiroshima" just like they failed to stop 9/11.

I had already planned to run for President, because I saw the danger America is in by getting so far away from God, what with continuing abortion and now Massachusetts legalizing homosexual marriage. I know that judgement is coming on America, and that unless America gets back to God and His protection, something far worse than 9/11 is going to happen. I knew that President Bush, although he was right to take out Saddam Hussein who was indeed a danger to the United States, did not do the war correctly and continues not to do the things necessary to win the war, like stop Iran's massive interference, and Syria's interference, and get truly adequate troop strength. I knew President Bush and Congress, including many Republicans, were failing to secure our borders, and stop the illegal invasion of our country by illegal immigrants. I see that diplomacy and sanctions are not going to stop Iran from getting nuclear weapons, and we know that Ahmadinejad has sworn to destroy Israel (which he calls "the Little Satan" and America (which he calls "the Big Satan"). If we do not take out Iran's 24 nuclear sites soon (my friend, General Tom McInerney, says we can do it in a 48 hour bombing attack), Iran will eventually start nuclear World War III and 200 million people could die. Don't you wish we had listened to Winston Churchill before World War II when he begged us to stop Hitler before he got big, but we waited until Hitler got big and then 62 million people had to die before we could stop him? It will be far, far worse if we wait until Ahmadinejad gets nukes.

So I saw America in perilous trouble, and the politicians are not doing any thing to stop the disaster that is coming. And when Dr. Williams and I learned that Osama was planning to devastate America with nuclear attacks in the near future, I knew I had to act. So I am using my life savings to run for President, to get out the message the Lord has put on my heart, that we must pass a Pro-Life Amendment and a Pro-Marriage Amendment, and stop abortion, and homosexual marriage, and get America back to God and His protection, or else we face disaster. And we must take out Iran's nuclear sites and Ahmadinejad and the Mullah's headquarters before they get nukes. And that will allow Iraq to settle down finally, without Iran's massive interference (and we must also stop Syria from allowing suicide bombers to enter Iraq from Syria). And so I decided to run for President. I truly believe I am the only candidate who will do the things necessary to save America from destruction.

Appendix Sixth Article

Cort for President 2008 Campaign Brochure

I am a lifelong Republican and a member of the President's Club of the Republican National Committee.

I am a Christian conservative who believes in traditional family values. I strongly support a Pro-Life Amendment to the U.S. Constitution banning abortion and a Pro-Marriage Amendment stating that marriage is only between a man and a woman. I believe the IRS needs to be abolished and replaced with the Fair Tax.

I am not a politician and that's a good thing. Simply I am an American who wants to serve his country and make a difference for ourselves and our children. The politicians have let us down. I am a practicing physician of psychiatric medicine, as well as an internationally recognized counter-terrorism expert.

Make no mistake; I am not a single issue candidate. Obviously, counter-terrorism is one of my chief concerns, however there many other issues facing America. Another concern I have is we need to secure our borders to stop the illegal immigration into this country.

I'm a Republican and running for President because I believe in hard work, self-reliance, less government, the preservation of our Christian values. Furthermore I am a strong supporter and believer in the free enterprise system that has made America the envy of the world.

I invite you to visit my website, www.cortforpresident.com. If you agree I am the one "true conservative" in this race, then please join my campaign and vote for me.

I am running for President of the United States because the Lord has given me a very important message to give to America. This message is that America has lost its way and strayed far from God and His protection, with abortion, homosexual marriage, and many other sins, that destruction is coming on America a million times worse than 9/11.

I am a counter-terrorism expert and I work with Dr. Paul Williams, author of "Osama's Revenge: The Next 9/11" and "The Day of Islam: The Annihilation of America and the Western World." We have learned that Osama bin Laden has a plan which he calls "The American Hiroshima," where he blows up 7 to 10 American cities with suitcase nukes. There is a strong possibility he has already smuggled these bombs through the porous Mexican border and they are here, possibly hidden in mosques in the cities he has targeted. We want the FBI to search inside these mosques.

Another reason I am running for President is to push for "The McInerney Plan". My friend. General Tom McInerney, Fox News military analyst, says we will never win the War in Iraq until we deal with Iran. The reason being Iran is actively involved in fighting against our troops with high tech IEDs called EFPs (explosively formed penetrators).

General McInerney goes on to say that Iran will have nuclear weapons in a year or less, and diplomacy and sanctions are obviously not going to work. He says we need to take out Iran's 24 nuclear sites and Ahmadinejad and the Mullahs' headquarters, and that we can do so in a 48 hour bombing campaign. Then the moderates in Iraq can take their country back, things will finally settle down in Iraq, we will have stopped Iran from getting nuclear weapons and starting World War III, and we will immediately win 80% of the War on Terror because Iran does 80% of the world's terror attacks. Don't you wish we had listened to Winston Churchill when he begged us to stop Hitler before he got big?

Five Questions for America

1. Do you want to pass a Pro-Life Amendment and the Federal Marriage Amendment, and get America back to God, and get His blessing, and victory over the Islamic-terrorists who are planning to destroy us?

2. Do you want to stop Osama bin Laden's coming attack?

3. Do you want to win the War in Iraq?

4. Do you want to stop Iran from getting nuclear weapons and starting World War III where 200 million or more people may die?

5. Do you want to win the War on Terror?

If your answer to these questions is yes, then please vote for me. Dr. Hugh Cort for President!

The Issues

IRAQ WAR

There should be no debate; we need to win the war in Iraq. Let's adopt the McInemey Plan and stop Iran's interference, then send another 100,000 troops into Iraq and win the war.

ILLEGAL IMMIGRATION

President Eisenhower, who my grandfather Brigadier General Hugh Cort served on the Joint Chiefs of Staff with. deported over 80,000 illegal aliens in about a year. I will follow Eisenhower's example and deport illegal aliens, build a fence and allow border patrol agents to do their job and stop anyone trying to enter our country illegally.

PRO LIFE

As a Christian conservative I know abortion is wrong-1 am Pro-Life and a member of Physicians for Life. Not only will I fight to get Roe v. Wade overturned; I will fight to pass an amendment banning abortion.

GAY MARRIAGE

Gay marriage is wrong. Marriage is God's Holy Sacrament between a man and a woman. I will fight for passage of the Federal Marriage Amendment.

TAX REFORM

It's time to abolish the IRS and replace the tax code with a simple, fair system. I strongly support the Fair Tax.

BALANCE THE BUDGET

The massive pork spending of Congress is shocking- As President I will veto every pork spending bill until Congress gets it through their heads that pork is dead. We <u>will</u> balance the budget!

Appendix Seventh Article

Osama Also Targeting London, Paris, Rome and other European Cities for Nuclear Attack

There is evidence that Osama bin Laden plans to detonate suitcase nuclear bombs in London, Paris, Rome, Copenhagen, and in 7 to 10 cities in the U.S. in the near future. Hamid Mir, the top Pakistani journalist who interviews Condoleeza Rice, Tony Blair, and Musharraf, and who has also interviewed Osama bin Laden three times, and who is the only man who has interviewed Osama after 9/11, reports that Osama has acquired suitcase nuclear bombs stolen from the former Soviet Union and is targeting London, Paris, Rome and other European cities, as well as American cities, in his "American Hiroshima" nuclear attack plan. Hamid Mir traced a nuclear suitcase bomb as far as Rome, Italy before he lost contact with his source (see "Al Qaeda's Hidden Arsenal: Interview with Hamid Mir" in the must-read articles section on the homepage of www.afcpr.org).

A year ago Osama came out with an audiotape where he said Europe will receive "a severe reaction" for re-publishing the cartoon about Mohammed. Osama said, "They (meaning Europeans) will see it (the severe reaction) but not hear it." When Osama says, "They will see it, but not hear it", he is referring to a nuclear blast, where people will see the flash of the nuclear explosion, but will be incinerated before they have time to hear the sound.

Now Osama has come out with a new audiotape threatening retaliation on European countries, including England, for assisting America in Afghanistan.

Osama bin Laden's youngest son, who many call Osama's "heir apparent", was recently on an Al Qaeda website reading his poem, where he says soon we will see the destruction of America, England, France, Italy, and Denmark.

Iran has been assisting Osama. One of Supreme Leader Khamenei's top advisors, Hassan Abassi, said last year, "We Iranians have devised a strategy for the destruction of Anglo-Saxon Civilization, and we know how we are going to attack them. "British Intelligence MI 6 in 2006 said that six of Pakistan's nuclear scientists, who helped Pakistan get the nuclear bomb, have been helping Iran develop the nuclear bomb, and they have also been assisting Osama bin Laden with his nuclear program, "advising Al Qaeda on how to weaponize fissionable materials it has now obtained," with the permission of Ahmadinejad.

Endnotes

1   ABC News, "October Surprise", September, 2008.... Also, Eli Lake, New York Sun, "Spies Warn That Al Qaeda Aims for October Surprise" September 22, 2008.

2   Al-Quds Al-Arabi newspaper, front page, Nov. 9, 2008.

3   Paul Williams, The Al Qaeda Connection: International Terrorism, Organized Crime, and the Coming Apocalypse, pg. 97.

4   Ibid., pg. 93.

5   Yossef Bodansky, Chechen Jihad: Al Qaeda's Training Ground and the Next Wave of Terror, pgs. 102-105.

6   Paul Williams, The Day of Islam: The Annihilation of America and the Western World, pgs. 163-165.

7   Paul Williams, Osama's Revenge: The Next 9/11: What the Media and the Government Haven't told You, pg. 138.

8   George Tenet, At the Center of the Storm: The CIA During America's Time of Crisis, pg. 264.

9   Gordon Thomas, "British Intelligence Confirms Al Qaeda Nukes", World Net Daily, 2006.

10 Paul Williams, The Al Qaeda Connection, pgs. 161, 163. Also The Day of Islam, pgs. 153-157.

11 David Dionisi, American Hiroshima: The Reasons Why and a Call to Strengthen America's Democracy, pgs. 6-9.

12 Ibid., pg. 4.

13 Ibid. pg. 3.

14 Stephen Younger, The Bomb: A New History, pg.158.

15 Paul Williams, The Day of Islam, pg. 166.

16 Steve Coll, The New Yorker Magazine, March 12, 2007.

17 David Dionisi, American Hiroshima, pg. 2.

18 Paul Williams, The Day of Islam, pgs. 209-210.

19 David Dionisi, American Hiroshima, pgs. 8-9.

20 Ibid., pg. 4.

21 Paul Williams, The Day of Islam, pgs. 201-202.

22 Paul Williams, The Al Qaeda Connection, pg. 165.

23 Ibid., pg.165.

24 Ibid., pg. 166.

25 Ibid., pg. 167.

26 Ibid., pg. 168.

27 Ibid., pg. 169.
28 Paul Williams, <u>The Day of Islam,</u> pgs. 168 – 169.
29 Paul Williams, <u>The Al Qaeda Connection,</u> pg. 169.
30 Paul Williams, <u>The Day of Islam,</u> pgs. 207 – 208.
31 Parade Magazine, March 4, 2007, pg. 15.
32 Paul Williams, <u>The Day of Islam,</u> pg. 82.